WHISPERS
in the
PINES

WHISPERS
in the
PINES
The Secrets of Colliers Mills

KAREN F. RILEY

KFR
Communications, LLC

Whispers in the Pines: The Secrets of Colliers Mills

First edition copyright © 2005 by Karen F. Riley
Published by Cloonfad Press, Cassville, NJ

Second edition copyright © 2009 by Karen F. Riley
Illustrations copyright © by Andrew Gioulis
Cover art copyright © by Andrew Gioulis
Cover photograph copyright © by Andrew Gioulis
Book design by Andrew Gioulis

Photographs of the author and illustrator copyright © Rich Schaub
Photography. Used by permission.

Published by: KFR Communications, LLC
            148 Hawkin Rd
            New Egypt, NJ 08533

Publisher's Note: The author and publisher have taken care in preparation
of this book but make no expressed or implied warranty of any kind and
assume no responsibility for errors or omissions. No liability is assumed for
incidental or consequential damages in connection with or arising out of
the use of the information contained herein.

ISBN-10: 0-6153-2521-1
ISBN-13: 978-0-615-32521-7

Printed in the United States of America

www.kfrcommunications.com

This book is dedicated to the memory of "Gramps"

Contents

Preface

Sometimes, we need an epiphany to make us take stock of what's really important in our lives, as in the movie, *Jerry McGuire.*

A few years ago, I became involved in an effort to save a piece of property from development. Although I had lived across the street from the parcel for eight years, all I knew of it was the farm field I saw from my window. I knew it bordered Colliers Mills Wildlife Management Area and that hunters often shot white tail deer that dashed across the field into the wooded area.

I had taken my son and his Boy Scout troop on a guided tour of Colliers Mills and had walked or driven there many times. But like Jerry McGuire, I saw only what I was ready to see at that point.

Colliers Mills, to me at that time, was sprawling unmarked habitat, densely populated with pitch pines and scrub oak and dotted with manmade lakes and dams. Its trails had never been officially marked and a pine-needled road could quickly turn into a sugar sand trap for those who ventured in without four-wheel drive...

But when I took a deeper study of the area to document species in my attempt to preserve the land from development, I discovered a parallel universe to ours – in some cases too small to be viewed without magnification, too camouflaged to be seen unless you knew how to be search, too silent to be heard unless one took the time to sit quietly and listen.

I tried to put the stress of juggling a full-time job, family life and night school behind me as I boldly walked across the field, basking in the golden sunshine of an early summer morning. As I stepped into the tree line, the temperature dropped, the air became heavy with a musky pine smell and an eerie silence filled the air. I paused at this quiet, majestic world – no ringing telephones, people arguing, clatter of technology. Just silence...

As I stood breathing in the earthy scent and adjusting my eyes to the densely shaded growth of trees, I began to hear birds. At first, it was just the call of a crow and a blue jay hopping closer to check me out. But then, slowly, the chattering picked up from the canopy of trees as birds flew from branch to branch. As I stood, craning my neck up at the ninety year old oak trees, the sounds became almost deafening – a well orchestrated chorus of catbirds, chickadees and cuckoos. As my breathing slowed and the tension ran from my muscles, I heard it...

Off in the distance, by the boggy marsh came the unmistakable twang of the green frog. It's like the sound of a rubber band snapping or the pluck of a banjo. First, one frog, then another, calling from a few hundred yards away. Soon, the tempo increased and a third joined the chorus.

I headed toward the lake to see if I could spot the usually well-camouflaged frogs. I stepped out onto the marshy ground that had once been a dam and a slight breeze rippled the glistening surface. In the deepest parts, it was a tea colored mirror, reflecting back the tall boughs and dotting of pine cones that bordered the lake. Along the edges, where the water was shallow, delicate mosses and white flowers poked through the surface.

I watched as a dragonfly landed on a nearby blueberry bush, its lacy wings catching the sunlight. More frogs had joined the chorus and a catbird was signaling my presence on a nearby maple.

And I smiled. The peace, the serenity that filled me – I felt as if I could stand here forever, taking it all in with my senses – and forget about the stress, the deadlines and the responsibilities that I had been burdened with only hours before.

I realized the irony that this had been here all this time – but virtually unknown to the motorist whizzing by on his way to work or the occasional runner who jogged along its edges.

Lacy flowers, moths smaller than your thumbnail, ridged fungi growing on the sides of tree trunks – it was all here and had been for years – yet most people never know of its existence.

I brought many people from all walks of life into this area and as they stepped into the tree line, they were overcome with wonder as I was. Careful not to disturb the plant life or disrupt the wildlife's activities, we quietly tiptoed through the woods and drank in the tranquility of this raw land.

For those who do not have the time, inclination, or ability to step into an area such as this and awaken your senses, this book is for you. May your shoulders relax, your breathing slow and your mind open with the beauty of nature that is unseen by most.

Come with me now, if you will, and view the jewel of the Pine Barrens...

How This Book Came About...

Quite frankly, this book came out by accident. Although I have been writing professionally since age eleven, it was for the magazine and newspaper trade. It had always been my desire to write a book. I had no idea what that book would be, but I felt I would know it when I found it.

In trying to prevent a housing development from being built on a pristine piece of land bordering Colliers Mills Wildlife Management Area on two sides, I spent five years doing research on the area. I discovered villages that had risen and fallen here and famous folk who once walked the same trails I now did. And I realized these were stories that had to be told. I had found my book.

In reality, the Pine Barrens had found me; although I didn't know it at the time. I fought the development, had the application unanimously overturned by the planning board, saw it appealed in court – all the while researching and putting together this book. On May 20, 2005 this book was released on the market. It was also the day that developers broke ground on the land that birthed this book. It was a bittersweet irony.

The late anthropologist, Margaret Mead, once said, "Never doubt that a small group of thoughtful, committed citizens can change the world. Indeed, it is the only thing that ever has."[1]

If my neighbors hadn't banded together with me and spoke up at township meetings, more houses would have been built. We got the number of units cut down and ten acres were deeded back to the township; the section bordering Colliers Mills. It was a small victory, but a victory nonetheless.

Since that time, I have given numerous book talks and signings for *Whispers in the Pines: The Secrets of Colliers Mills.* I encourage people to become educated about the things they value, speak up for what they believe in and know that even one person can make a difference. It all has to start somewhere.

Those who came to my signings and talks sent me feedback and encouraged me to keep speaking out. During that time, they championed me as a spokesperson for the Pines. It was a title I had not earned.

But the fires had been stoked. The little knowledge I had gained during the five years of research begged for more in-depth study. The folks I talked to wanted to hear more. And my husband, Bill, who came to my inaugural book signing and talk, listened to the crowd's comments and suggested I consider writing about the people of the Pine Barrens.

This book was about the history and environment of Colliers Mills, the northern end of the Pine Barrens. But the Pine Barrens consists 1.1 million acres; and only 12, 652 belong to Colliers Mills, which left a vast footprint for me to still explore.

And not everyone enjoys reading about history. But all of us can relate to people. So I ventured back into the woods I had started to fall in love with and tell the history of the Pine Barrens through the eyes of the people who lived and worked there. Almost four years later – on April 17, 2009, *Voices in the Pines: True Stories from the New Jersey Pine Barrens* by Plexus Publishing, hit the marketplace.

It has been a labor of love. And while uncovering "secrets" from other areas of the Pines, I learned that there was still more to be uncovered here in Colliers Mills. I learned about how a group of concerned citizens and politicians prevented 15,000 drums of radium-contaminated soil from being deposited in Colliers Mills. I did not know anything of the story when I wrote *Whispers*, but I covered it extensively in my second book, including public documents and other information that had never appeared in the newspapers. I felt fortunate that people trusted me enough to share their stories and information with me so others could become educated.

My information also came from unlikely sources, such as reviews on my first book. From Ben Ruset, webmaster of njpinebarrens.com, I learned about the "hermit of La-Ha-Way." The hermit – J. Turner Brakeley – was the only child of John Howell Brakeley, D.D., a Methodist preacher and proprietor of the now defunct Bordentown Female College. It seems that the son fell in love with a student of the college and had plans to marry her after he passed the bar exam. However, the groom-to-be unwittingly caught his girl in the arms of another and moved into buildings on the Lahaway cranberry bog plantations that his father owned.[2]

There he lived out his life as a recluse, studying constellations, plants and insects and recording his findings in journals. At one time, Princeton University had exhibits on his study of wasps. Brakeley was also said to have cultivated many varieties of water lilies[3]; a fact I find interesting since the water lilies covering the ponds at Colliers Mills were one of the first things that captured my attention. Brakely was born on January 10, 1847 and died near Bordentown on August 24, 1915.[4]

I am thankful for Ben educating me on Brakeley and writing the foreword for this revised edition of *Whispers*. There are many unsung heroes and heroines of the Pine Barrens who are far more knowledgeable sources of Pine Barrens lore and I'm honored that they have encouraged and supported my writings.

In April of 2010, my third book on the Pine Barrens is scheduled to be released by Arcadia Publishing. It will contain vintage photos and information on other areas of the Pine Barrens I am exploring and learning about.

Since the initial release of *Whispers*, many other things have changed. My original publisher has gone out of business and the first edition went out of print. Because so many have continued to request it – of which I am very grateful – I have decided to bring out a new edition.

I thought about updating the content to include Brakely and the radon battle, but in the end, decided to stick to the stories that the public has told me they have enjoyed. So the text is mainly in its original form, with some "freshening up" of some minor content and updates.

I decided to reintroduce *Whispers* with brand new illustrations and a cover design by someone who has developed a real heart for the pines as well; my business partner, Andrew Gioulis. Andrew did the front cover and inside illustrations for *Voices* and I'm sure that he will delight you with his work here as well in this new release of *Whispers*. If you haven't already, may you come to love the Pines as much as we have…

Acknowledgements

First and foremost, I have to thank my readers. It was your feedback to my first book that spawned the second. And it was your requests that prompted me to reintroduce *Whispers in the Pines: The Secrets of Colliers Mills* to audiences once more, enhancing and improving the new version while still preserving the original manuscript that you responded so favorably to.

I have dedicated this book to "Gramps." My grandfather taught me to be patient with nature and to listen to what is unheard by most. It is not easy to keep a rambunctious eight-year-old quiet while walking in the woods, but I quickly learned the rewards of doing so as I watched him commune with nature. It was in those early days that my love of the land was kindled.

Gramps lived to the ripe age of eighty-nine, leaving behind a legacy of wonderful memories and a life richly lived. He immigrated to this country when he was only sixteen years old. He came alone, leaving family, friends and the only life he had ever known behind. He knew very few words in English and when he was asked his name at Ellis Island, he replied, "John J. Kaiser." He was asked what the middle initial stood for and not understanding the question, thought his response had not been heard clearly and so he repeated, "John." And so he went through the remainder of his life as "John John" and none ever knew what his real middle name was. He had left part of his identity behind to start afresh in this new land.

Gramps had grown up on a farm and without much formal education; he set about working with his hands, first as a tailor and then a woodcrafter. As a child, I was in awe when I learned the beautifully carved desk and breakfront, with its intricate scrollwork and patterns, had been made from scratch by him.

He later became a bartender, which remained his employ until he retired. He worked at Feltzman's, a famous restaurant on the boardwalk at Coney Island. The amusement area was in its heyday and my grandfather became famous for being able to carry the most glasses on his forearm, deftly balancing the drinks without the use of a tray. But his family relished the trinkets he would bring home from beach goers who left items at the bar after a few too many imbibes. There was quite a collection of transistor radios, and one time, a man even left behind his kitten!

But what I will always remember best about Gramps is the special time he and I shared on long walks in the parks near our house. He bought me my first ice cream cone and being very small at the time and unfamiliar with this confection, I promptly started with the bottom of the cone and much to my dismay, ended up with the ice cream all over me instead of in me! I remember Gramps being upset, because the cone had cost twenty-five cents of his hard-earned money and his generation never wasted or wanted for anything.

In the fall, we would make a detour to the supermarket, scooping up bags of raw nuts. Then we'd head down to the park along the water's edge, laden with our delicious treats. We'd pick a quiet spot under a sprawling oak tree and then the magic would begin. I'd watch as my grandfather quietly bent down, a peanut in his outstretched hand. Slowly, deliberately, a squirrel would make its way down the tree and over to his hand. Never taking his eyes off my grandfather, the squirrel would snatch the peanut from his hand. Gramps would laugh and put a fresh peanut on his palm and soon the squirrel would be back. More squirrels would come, each taking their turn.

He encouraged me to do it, but I was never still enough for the squirrels to trust me. For hours, I would watch him feed the squirrels. He told me how important it was that we gave the squirrels nuts to store away over the winter so they would not get hungry and die. As an adult, reflecting back and realizing that shortly after my grandfather settled down and starting earning money, the Great Depression hit, made me look at these moments in a new light.

I smile when I look at the illustration of the squirrel in the revised edition of *Whispers*, because it gives me a chance to revisit these wonderful far off memories that have been tucked out of reach for so long. Bringing this book out again gave us the chance to create new pen-and-ink drawings of the amazing flora and fauna of this area. Perhaps they will spur memories of your own.

And for these, I have to thank Andrew Gioulis, an award-winning graphic designer and illustrator. He meticulously researched the species we chose to illustrate in this book, making sure the specific characteristics were represented accurately. Andrew's work brought the stories of the people of the Pine Barrens alive in *Voices in the Pines,* and I'm grateful that he worked with me on the illustrations and cover design of *Whispers,* as well.

Friends are truly the flowers of the earth. Brilliant, unassuming, constant – they know you better than you know yourself at times. True friends challenge you to be more than you ever thought you could be and then push you to greater heights. And when you stumble, they know how to help regain your momentum and not wallow in self-pity. I truly would not be here today without the help of these incredible people. And so it is fitting that I acknowledge their loyalty: Maryann Kley, Maureen McCarthy, Rita Balducci, Cecilia Cross, Lisa Sarubbi, Gloria Stevens, Jamileh DiGuida, the late Anne Corda, Jeanne Palomino, Diane Caprioglio, Mary Brybag, and so many others, who have touched my life in so many ways.

For those seeking to become a writer, or improve your craft – I urge you to find a local writers group. The feedback, motivation and suggestions can greatly improve your skills. I have belonged to several groups, but the Jackson Writers Group has proven to be a wellspring of support and encouragement. My gratitude to Janet Fair, Larry

Meegan, Karen Kelly Boyce, Pat Dunkin, Alison DeLuca, Jim Lair and Linda Krupey. These original members watched this book take shape. Since then, many new members have joined and their works proudly line the shelves of stores and libraries, where it all began.

In researching this book, a number of people stepped to the plate and volunteered their time and knowledge. Their extraordinary efforts must be acknowledged: Conservation Officer Dominick Fresco, who is assigned to Colliers Mills Wildlife Management Area and spent considerable time providing me with detailed information; geologist Rich Bizub of the Pinelands Preservation Alliance, whose guidance on geology and the water table was invaluable; arborist Mark Vodak, who painstakingly helped identify trees for me; and Dr. Michael Gross, Director of the Arboretum at Georgian Court College, who along with field botanists Linda Kelly and Karl Anderson, spent countless hours helping identify plants and enriched my limited knowledge of flora.

Last but certainly not least, comes the first place ribbon for my husband, Bill and our three children – Lisa, Laura and Christopher. Nothing would have ever gotten written if you did not pitch in with the chores, get dinner on the table and honor the request of silence while I proofread and gathered my thoughts. Families give each other strength; they also make the ultimate sacrifice for the greater good and to see their loved ones succeed. Bill has truly been the "wind beneath my wings" – standing in the shadows, basking in my success – often at the cost of his own freedom and desires.

I'd like to ask you to think of those individuals in your life who have shaped your destiny. Take a moment to thank them and let them know the value they hold in your life. If there is one lesson above any other that has been impressed upon me while writing this book, it is this: Life is short. We never know what tomorrow holds. Treasure what you have, as it – or you – may not be here the next day. Life is a gift from God; use it wisely and appreciate what you have been given.

Foreword

The area near where Burlington, Monmouth, and Ocean counties meet is a strange and wondrous place. Take a drive down any one of the many sugar sand roads that crisscross the region and the forest seems to swallow you up. The air gets noticeably heavy - and, in the hot summer months, fragrant with the smell of pine. Pitch pines, scrub oaks, and maples line the roads, some charred from the fires that sweep through the region. With the exception of hunters who come during deer season, the area is usually vacant.

This is the land of Colliers Mills, on the northern fringes of the New Jersey Pine Barrens. Bordered by Lakehurst Naval Air Center to the south, Fort Dix to the southwest, and Manchester, Plumsted and Jackson to the north and east, the area around Colliers Mills looks much as it was over one hundred years ago, despite the ever present threat of development.

The buzzing of sawmill blades and the fragrance of smoldering wood, watched over carefully by the colliers, eager to sell their charcoal to the nearby iron furnaces, once filled the air. Here fortunes were made and lost, and dreams and hopes flourished in the idyllic countryside.

Now all that remains of Colliers Mills, the settlement, are a few old buildings - some in ruins, the name kept alive only in the name of one of the largest Wildlife Management Areas in the state. Many who speed through the area may look quickly at the woods passing by and think the area desolate. One old map from 1795 labels the southern part of New Jersey – in letters that stretch from Cape May to Freehold – "an extensive forest of pine trees." Adjectives such as "wasteland" and "barren" have frequently been ascribed to this area.

Stop, though, for a moment along one of the lonely sand roads in Colliers Mills and take in your surroundings. So attuned to modern life are we – cars racing by, airplanes overhead, phones ringing – that the absence of those sounds is eerie.

Then, you'll discover much like the author did, that you begin to notice the chorus of frogs, and screech from some far away hawk. Delve a little bit further and you'll begin to see the diversity in the area. Pines and oaks give way to cedar and maple. In hidden clearings orchids grow. Colliers Mills is a naturalists' dream.

I have been exploring the area for over ten years and have yet to really scratch the surface. I've been lost in the gloomy stretches of cedar swamp in the southern part of the WMA, and scratched my head as I've examined ruins of buildings deep in the woods, wondering about the types of people who once called this place home.

The secrets of Colliers Mills are whispered through the trees. Karen Riley and this book are your guides for exploring them. Even if you don't get a chance to visit, you'll get a sense of the serenity and majesty of this jewel of the Pine Barrens.

- Ben Ruset,
Founder of www.njpinebarrens.com

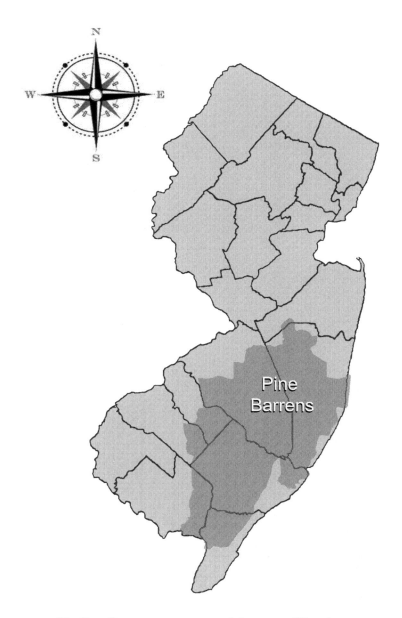

The Pine Barrens occupy 22% of the state of New Jersey.

At present, Colliers Mills Wildlife Management Area consists of 12, 652 acres and is the northernmost part of the Pine Barrens.

The History of Colliers Mills

She teetered on the edge. From this height, she had a birds-eye view of the lush green canopy of pine and oak stretched out before her in all directions.

The wind tugged at her clothes. Adrenalin must have been coursing through her veins as she looked at the ground, one hundred-fifteen feet below her.

Would she jump? *Courage is the price that life exacts for granting peace,* she believed.[5] No one would stop her.

As she fell, drifting past the treetops, her parachute opened. Safely, it carried her to the ground. It was June 2, 1935 and history had just been made. Amelia Earhart was the first public person to jump from the tower erected by her husband, George Palmer Putnam, and Stanley Switlik.

She strongly believed that women should do for themselves what men had already done – and occasionally what men had not done – to establish themselves as persons and encourage other women toward greater independence of thought and action.[6]

It was this philosophy that drove her to break records soaring above the clouds. She knew the hazards of attempting what had never been done before. She did not let that stop her.

As she glided toward the earth that day, she joined a long line of pioneers that had boldly chartered firsts on this land. It was not just a pine and oak forest that Amelia had landed in that day but an area steeped in history.

Stanley Switlik had built his one hundred-fifteen foot tower to train airmen in parachute jumping. It stood on his property in the northwestern section of Jackson Township in Ocean County, New Jersey.

Switlik, a Russian immigrant of Polish-Ukrainian descent, came to America in 1907 in the steerage compartment. He was only sixteen years old when he arrived at Ellis Island.

He worked at a number of odd jobs until 1920, when he bought a canvas and leather manufacturing company with the help of relatives and friends. The Canvas-Leather Specialty Company, as it came to be called, manufactured coal bags, pork roll casings and mailbags for the Post Office.

It evolved into the Switlik Parachute Company, designing flight clothing, gunner belts and parachutes. By 1930, it had become the country's largest parachute manufacturer.

In December of 1941, the United States government ordered a few parachute makers, including Switlik, to increase production by fifty percent. Switlik's company met the demand and was given an Army-Navy "E" Award in 1942 for its manufacturing effort.[7]

The Switlik Parachute Company made Switlik quite wealthy and he used that money to purchase property from the township that had been taken as tax liens. He paid roughly a dollar an acre for the land and later donated much of it to the State at the request of Lester G. MacNamara, Superintendent of Wildlife Management, New Jersey Division of Fish and Game.

The State undertook a massive reconstruction project of the land they later renamed Colliers Mills Wildlife Management Area. The majority of funding came from the Pittman-Robertson program, which was started in 1938 as an excise tax on sporting arms. The remaining costs were borne by hunting license fees.

On October 13, 1951, the State dedicated Lake Success – the largest of the Colliers Mills lakes – in a public ceremony attended by Switlik. Other honored guests at the dedication included Dr. A. Heaton Underhill, the Director of the Division of Fish and Game, who served as Master of Ceremonies; Albert M. Day, Chief of the United States Fish and Wildlife Service and Alfred E. Driscoll, Governor of New Jersey at that time.

The group assembled on the dam where the original mill once operated. Colliers Mills had come full circle, from the days when the Indians hunted and fished here to a wildlife area where hunters and fisherman would again come.

Frank J. Valgenti, Chairman of the State Division of Fish and Game, summed it up to the numerous sportsmen and women gathered there by saying, "The restoration of this lake will add greatly to the enjoyment of our people, whether to hunt, fish or swim, or whether just to wander along its banks in these pine lands, so rich in the lore of New Jersey's early days."

The Paleo-Indians were the first hunters of Colliers Mills. They hunted mastodon, mammoth, caribou and musk ox, killing them with crude projectiles. They ate the meat and fashioned the skin and bones into tents and clothing.

As glaciers melted and temperatures rose, it is believed the Paleo-Indians moved north, following the mammals that headed toward the colder climate for which they were better adapted.

Other Native Americans moved into the region. Archaeological digs have revealed that the aborigines added nuts, berries and roots to their diet and cooked over open fires. They also clammed, fished and used spears to hunt game. They cut down trees and constructed canoes.

After the decline of the aborigines, the area was populated with the Lenni Lenape Indian tribe, also referred to as the Lenape of the Delaware. They were part of a larger tribe called the Algonkian Indians. The Algonkian tribe stretched across the northeastern United States and eastern Canada.

In New Jersey, the Lenape were further divided into three families. The family that populated the Colliers Mills area was called the Unilatchigo. They were a gentle people, who welcomed others to their land.

They hunted elk, fished and farmed. From tracking the elk, they learned where shelter and water were and set up villages nearby. They also traveled and traded with other tribes in the region. Ornamental items made from materials like soapstone have been unearthed which are not native to this area.

The Lenape believed they had been placed here as "Keepers of the Land and Water" and treated the earth with respect. They utilized every part of the animals they hunted. They had no concept of personal wealth or private property and shared what they had when the Europeans arrived.

On July 12, 1734, Indian John Pombelous sold his tract of land, which in part became Colliers Mills, to Edmund Beakes and his heirs for thirty shillings. Six others in the tribe and colonists Thomas Cobbs, James Frazee and Anthony Woodward witnessed the deed signed by Edmund Beakes and Indian John Pombelous. It assigned the land, water, hunting rights and all mines and quarries that existed on the land.

It is believed the Native Americans thought the shillings offered by the Europeans were their way of sharing what they had and did not realize they had actually "sold" their land to them in exchange for the coins until they were forced off the land. By 1758, there were only a few hundred Lenape left in the state.

In February of that year, representatives of the State and of the Lenape met to resolve conflicting land claims. Out of that meeting grew the Treaty of Crosswicks, which established 3,044 acres of land in Burlington County as the only Indian reservation in New Jersey. At the time it was called Brotherton; today it is known as Indian Mills.

The reservation had a school, a gristmill, a trading store, a meeting-house and a blacksmith shop.[8] But the land was not productive and the Indians were harassed by the local colonists who allowed their herds to graze on the reservation.

In 1801, the remaining sixty-three residents of Brotherton sold the land back to the State and used part of the funds to relocate to New Stockbridge, New York, with the Mahican Indian tribe. The rest of the money was used to purchase clothing, equipment and furnishing; with the remainder invested in U.S. securities.

In 1822, forty of the Brotherton Indians moved to Green Bay, Michigan by using the securities money. Ten years later, they were in financial difficulty and appealed to seventy-six year old Lenape Bartholomew S. Calvin for help. Calvin appeared before the New Jersey State Legislature on March 12, 1832, offering to relinquish the hunting and fishing rights of the Brotherton land that had not been included in the 1801 settlement.

His moving speech, which said in part, "...not a drop of blood have you spilled in battle – not an acre of our land have you taken but by our consent..." provided the Indians with a $2,000 settlement and ended their ties with New Jersey.

The town that grew up by Success Lake was called Success Mills. The land included a cedar swamp called Covinshannoc Creek by the Indians. It is now known as Shannoc Brook. Morgan's Branch and Borden's Branch flowed into the Covinshannoc and then into Success Lake on its eastern side. It is here that Beakes built his sawmill, using the force of the water to operate it.

Since the Lenape had taken such good care of the land, only cutting down what they needed, the area was full of hardwood to support the sawmill industry.

Another mill by the name of Shreves Mill also operated in this area. Shreves Mill was later purchased by John Collier who continued to operate the sawmill. Some credit the name of "Colliers Mills" to this mill, but the more widely accepted version is that the name sprung from the activities of colliers, or charcoal makers. Charcoal mining was spawned by another industry, the production of bog iron. Charcoal was made from charring wood in a homemade kiln, which was then used as the source or "coal" to smelt bog iron, hence the name, "charcoal."

It took almost four cords of wood to make one hundred bushels of charcoal. After the cords of wood were cut, a pole called a "fergen" was placed in the center of the newly cleared field, with short lengths of wood stacked around it, in a teepee-like fashion. Layers of turf were packed onto the sides to prevent air from escaping. Sand was then poured over the turf to further seal the kiln.

The cords of wood were dropped into the top of the kiln along with ignited kindling until they almost reached the opening. The kiln was watched by a "collier" or charcoal maker. He would place a ladder against the side to check on the fire's intensity at least once an hour.

The collier would poke air holes into the bottom of the kiln. He watched the color of the smoke that escaped from the holes. If the smoke was blue, the fire was burning too hot and he would plug some of the holes with sand. If the fire was too hot, the wood would burn instead of char. The color of the smoke would also let him know when the charring process was complete.

Colliers stayed in the woods by the kilns for the entire two weeks that it took to complete the process. They would even sleep along-side them so they could closely watch the fires. When the charcoal was done, the collier poured sand into the opening to extinguish the flames and push out any remaining air. Charcoal was highly combustible and exposing it to air could cause the entire kiln to explode.

The coals were gradually cooled and packaged for shipment out of the area if they were not going to be used locally for bog iron. Mules would pull specially designed boxes - indigenous to New Jersey - that would permit the coal to be dumped easily on the ground when it reached its final destination. A wagon carting improperly cooled charcoal could burst into flame on its journey.

An experienced collier could watch up to twenty kilns at a time. Charcoal mining continued into the 20th century in Ocean County, with the last kiln extinguished in 1976 in Manchester Township.

From 1760 to 1860, the smelting of bog iron was another major industry in the Pine Barrens. Bog iron is believed to be the first iron ore ever mined, starting around 2,000 B.C. in Europe. Norseman from Scandinavia used bog iron for helmets, weapons, tools and for repairing their boats.

The first record of bog iron mining in New Jersey was the Tinton Falls Iron Works established in 1675.[9] However, this factory failed when nearby Hammersmith Works closed down. It wasn't until the French and Indian War and the Revolutionary Wars that the industry revived. Bog iron was used to make cannon balls. Production of Pinelands' bog iron peaked during the War of 1812.

In between the wars, iron was used to make pots, pans, fences, furniture, household decorations, nails, horseshoes, wagon tires and stoves.[10]

The chemical process of forming bog iron takes twenty to thirty years to complete. The still water of the pinelands' many bogs is edged with pitch pine trees. The acidity of the needles fall into the water and mix with the decaying vegetation on the swamp's clay bottom to yield a crude form of iron oxide, which rises to the water's surface. In many areas of the Pine Barrens, the bottom of the streambed is made of marl or greensand which contains iron. *Gallionella* and *Leptothrix* bacteria – which thrive in the acidic water – help change the iron oxide into a hard ore, referred to as "bog iron."

The bog iron was then collected from the swamps and transported to the furnace for smelting. The mining collection process destroyed the delicate wetlands surrounding the bogs, but if the water and soil conditions remained intact, the ore formation would begin anew.

Approximately thirty smelting furnaces for bog iron are known to have existed in the Pine Barrens. Villages would spring up where smelting furnaces were located. It was an ideal industry for the area as two other elements were needed for smelting: water power and fuel. Streams were dammed to provide power for the smelting machinery. Forests were cleared and burned for charcoal. Pine trees, in particular, would burn the ore at the correct intensity.

The smelting furnace was about three feet tall and one foot in diameter. It was made of stone lined with clay and circular in shape. The inner walls were lined with mortar, brick and sand to insulate the interior chamber. Leather bellows operating in pairs forced air into the furnace causing the temperature to rise as much as 2,400 degrees Fahrenheit. The air inside the furnace filled with carbon dioxide, pulling oxygen from the bog iron and transforming it into impure elementary iron.

The process took many hours to complete and used up a massive amount of charcoal. Two and a half tons of ore and one hundred and eighty bushels of charcoal were needed to produce one ton of iron.

The furnace had to be watched closely by the smelter. Some furnaces had shallow troughs carved into the floor where the iron would settle. These troughs were called "pigs" and the iron that resulted from it was called "pig iron" or cast iron.

By repeating the process, more impurities are removed. The iron also becomes more pliable, turning it into wrought iron. Blacksmiths used forge hammers that weighed over five hundred pounds to shape the iron. As they worked, the sound of their hammers would echo through the pines.

Founders oversaw the production – typically there were two founders per furnace, each working twelve hour shifts. Founders were responsible for the hiring and firing of the approximately sixty men needed per furnace. Under the founder were skilled or semi-skilled laborers called fillers or bankman, who loaded the furnace, and gutter-men and molders who handled the molten metal. Blacksmiths, pattern-makers and unskilled laborers rounded out the work force.

Numerous forges and furnaces sprung up throughout the Pine Barrens to meet the demand. The ironworkers toiled long hours and villages formed near the furnaces. The village of Success Mills is said to have prospered with dozens of families living there.

By 1840, the industry had peaked. As demand outpaced the supply, new sources had to be found and iron was imported from northern New Jersey and Staten Island.

Another source of iron surfaced which helped to end the Pinelands industry. Iron ore from stone beds in Pennsylvania yielded a purer grade of iron than the bogs in the Pinelands did. A smelting agent called anthracite proved to be more effective than charcoal and the iron ore beds in Pennsylvania were located near anthracite fields. Coal was also discovered near these beds in the 1840's.

Numerous fires destroyed the villages and mills in the Pinelands and costs to rebuild were too prohibitive. The bog industry was plagued with financial difficulties due to its low efficiency. As production decreased, furnaces were sold at tremendous losses. Gloucester Furnace near Egg Harbor sold for $50,000 in 1825, yet the land value alone counted for $35,000.

An editorial in the *Camden Mail and General Advertiser*, noted on July 1, 1840: "It is suggested that the recent application of anthracite fuel to the smelting of iron ore will be very injurious, if not fatal, to the iron works of New Jersey."[11] With the industry no longer viable in the Pine Barrens, the town of Success faded into the history books.

Wetlands, destroyed by years of bog iron mining, gave birth to a new industry: cranberry growing. The Lenape had been the first to use cranberries which they called "sasemineash" for food, medicine and dye. The settlers, upon seeing the spring blossoms of this vine, thought they looked like the head of a crane, so they called the fruit "crane berries".

**The stages of cranberry growth - from young plant to flower
(note how the flower resembles the head of a crane) and finally, fruit**

Legend has it that John "Peg Leg" Webb, a schoolteacher in Goshen, first noticed cranberry vines thriving in a swampy marsh. He used his wooden leg to poke holes in the swamp where he planted more vines. The produce from these artificially planted berries was far superior to that of the ones grown in the dry fields, higher up than the swampland.

Existing swamps were pressed into service as cranberry bogs. The stands of Atlantic White Cedar trees present in the swamps were cut down and the wood used for housing, boat building and fences. The stumps were left in the bogs and still can be seen throughout abandoned cranberry bogs in the Pinelands.

Harvesting cranberries was very labor intensive and the one-room schoolhouses of the time would close down during harvest time so children could help pick the berries by hand from the vine. Strips of cloth were wrapped around the workers' hands to protect them from scratches and cuts.

The workers would crawl across the fields on their hands and knees to pick the cranberries from the vines. At the end of the day, the cranberry pickers would gather around a campfire to dry out their soaked clothing and make up songs among the Pines.

Later, a cranberry scoop was invented that had metal or wooden teeth on the end that would pluck the cranberries from the vine and catch them in the base of the scoop. This considerably lessened the workers' hours. In the 1940's, with workers serving overseas in World War II, machinery was invented to replace the hand labor.

Sea captains brought cranberries by the barrelful on their ships to prevent scurvy. Cranberries are not only high in Vitamin C but are also less perishable than citrus fruit such lemons or limes.

Scurvy was known as the "plague of the sea" at that time due to the high mortality rates that resulted from long oceanic trips. Two-thirds of Vasco de Gama's crew perished in 1499 from scurvy during his voyage to India. Magellan lost more than eighty percent of his crew to the disease in 1520 while crossing the Pacific.[12]

Scurvy is caused by a Vitamin C deficiency. Vitamin C — known as ascorbic acid — aids in the synthesis of enzymes and amino acids used to produce collagen in the body. A lack of collagen causes the walls of the blood vessels to weaken and hemorrhaging occurs. Black-and-blue marks from internal bleeding appear on the skin. Lesions form on the skin where the capillaries of hair follicles have burst. Gums bleed and weaken and dentin, which is part of the root of teeth, breaks down.

James Lind, a physician on the HMS Salisbury, which sailed from England to the Plymouth Colony in 1747[13], first experimented with the diets of those on board suffering from scurvy. The crewmen who ate citrus fruit recovered from scurvy. In 1795, the British Royal Navy started offering a daily ration of lemon or lime juice to its crew. This is how the term "limey" for seaman was coined.[14]

An enterprising young man by the name of Ephraim Emson soon became known as the "Cranberry King" because of the vast number of cranberry bogs that he owned. Ephraim or "Eph" as he was called, was one of six children born to Captain Christian D. Emson of Schleswig, Denmark, and Lydia Potter. In some records, the surname is spelled "Empson" although "Emson" seems to be the more widely accepted version.

Captain Emson became a sailor before the age of ten and served in the First Napoleonic War. He met Napoleon a few times and described him as a "nice looking man with hands like a lady". Emson's father provided Napoleon with the mount he rode when he invaded Russia.

The captain was shipwrecked four times and the last time, he came ashore on New Jersey Beach, a few miles from the Toms River cemetery where he was later buried. In 1803, he erected a house that was described as "the most pretentious house on Main Street." It sat just above the ridge where Washington Street is today and had a clear view to the Toms River.

He soon commanded vessels that traded between New York and Toms River. Among those vessels were the schooners "Garrett Ellison," "Charles Rhine" and "Superior," which delivered iron ore from places such as Cold Spring, NY.

He became rather wealthy, sold his possessions around 1832 and moved his family to Highland County, Ohio. He farmed there for twelve years and then returned to New Jersey, this time settling in Freehold. He sold his land and possessions in Ohio at a profit and was able to start his son, Ephraim, off with a nice fortune. Captain Emson died on November 29, 1889, naming Ephraim as executor of his estate.

Young Ephraim took up real estate and farming, in addition to cranberry growing. Emson is said to have owned over 15,000 acres of land. The earliest existing index of deeds stored at the Toms River county clerk's office show one hundred-sixty properties that he held mortgages for, including property in Plumsted (spelled "Plumstead" at that time), Jackson, Stafford, Brick, Manchester, Dover, Lakewood and Barnegat, as well as land in Monmouth and Burlington counties. The deeds recorded range in date from July 20, 1854 to January 5, 1898.

In 1869, he married Sarah Elizabeth Allen. Sarah was the daughter of the ex-Sheriff of Perrineville, Charles Allen and his wife, Hannah W. Charles Allen was the owner of the general store in Goshen, later renamed Cassville, to honor General Lewis Cass. His store was on the southwest corner of what is now Routes 528 and 571, directly opposite the Cassville M.E. Church and the cemetery where he and his wife were later buried.

Allen, a democrat and a great admirer of Andrew Jackson, suggested the name of "Jackson" for the township to Dr. George Fort of New Egypt. Fort, a pharmacist, physician and the postmaster of New Egypt, credited himself in a letter written to the editor of the New Jersey Courier in 1866 with the separation of Jackson Township in March of 1844 and Plumsted (New Egypt) Township in 1845 from Monmouth County.

Fort wanted to name the township Johnson, after Colonel R. M. Johnson, but Judge Allen insisted upon "Jackson" and Fort finally agreed. Fort later became governor of the state.

Ephraim and Sarah had at least four children – two of which survived to adulthood – a daughter, Miss Hannah, born in 1872and a son, Christian D. (nicknamed "Budd"), born in April of 1877.

Emson became a member of the Democratic Party and quickly rose through the ranks to become a New Jersey Assemblyman in 1862 and 1876, a State Senator from 1878 to 1880, and a Lay Judge of the Ocean County courts from 1892 to 1896. He was considered for Congressional and Gubernatorial positions during his tenure.

He served thirty years as a Jackson freeholder and was a member of the Democratic State Executive Committee. A freeholder was someone who owned land that was free of debt. Their initial purpose was to negotiate deeds to construct county buildings.

As Ocean County's population swelled from 10,032 in 1850 to 13,707 only five years later, freeholder meetings were increased from being held on an annual basis to being held quarterly to accommodate the needs of a growing county. A century later, in 1950, Ocean County would become home to a population of 56,622, residing in thirty-three municipalities.

Despite his success in politics, Emson's real love was horses. He kept forty horses – all full-blooded stock – at his Colliers Mills estate. He even had a private racetrack built on the estate's property. He had a second, public racetrack built, the remains of which can still be seen in the woods on the western side of Hawkin Road.

The New Jersey Courier, dated December 15, 1869, told of a spirited harness race between Mr. Daniel Bigbee's bay mare, "Gimbleshanks" and Richard Gaskill's mare, "Susie Ann". Stakes were placed on the race and Gimbleshanks, favored to win, did not disappoint onlookers, winning two of the three half-mile heats.

This passion proved to be his downfall, as he was thrown from a cart pulled by one of his favorite horses, which was said to have been startled by a barking dog. Emson weighed over two hundred and fifty pounds and the fall broke five of his ribs, two of which pierced his right lung, causing him to hemorrhage to death two days later at his house. He was sixty years old.

During his lifetime, Emson contributed much to society. He built a one-room schoolhouse in 1857, which stood at the juncture of Colliers Mills and Woodruff Roads. The schoolhouse was later moved to the corner of Woodruff and Route 539, where it stands today, although it is now a private residence and has been considerably renovated.

Emson also paid for and built a Methodist Episcopalian Church, which stood next to the original schoolhouse. The last service is said to have been in 1923 and today a house stands on the spot where the church once stood.

His various businesses employed many from the area. When the Pennsylvania Railroad decided to stop running its train line from Pemberton to Hightstown, Emson stepped in to organize a company to lease and operate the railroad. He provided the financial backing to keep the line running for a number of years.

At the entrance to present day Colliers Mills on the left- alongside Colliers Mills Lake – stood a large three storied hotel built by Ephraim. Summer visitors who came to swim in the lake used the hotel. It had forty rooms, a ballroom and running water. In the yard were an icehouse and a windmill. On Saturday night, the villagers would gather in the ballroom to drink, dance and listen to Jersey pine fiddlers.

Across the lake was the General Store, which also served as a Post Office for General Delivery to Colliers Mills, meaning that the area residents would come here to pick up their mail. Emson was the Colliers Mills Postmaster.

Across the road stood two distilleries – one for making whiskey and the other for wintergreen oil. A stone building, used by the Division of Fish and Wildlife today as a storage shed, is believed to have been a large steam saw mill. When the state took over the land, they found a large saw blade in the building.

Underneath the dam that divides Colliers Mills Lake from Turnmill Pond is a water wheel, believed to power one of the mills. Emson owned a total of three sawmills and two gristmills.

He was buried in the Cassville cemetery, behind the Cassville United Methodist Church, which was built in 1859. The cemetery is the final resting place for a number of civil war veterans as well as John Truex, a Revolutionary War veteran who died in December of 1834.

In the center of the cemetery is a massive pine tree, towering over the Emson gravesite. Its top is broken, its mighty branches draped over the final resting place of Emson and his wife.

To the left of the gravesite are two slender cement crypts containing the couple's young daughters. Lizzie was born June 29, 1880 and died August 6, 1882, barely two years of age. Nellie, who is buried to the left of her sister, was born on November 2, 1872 and died on April 13, 1883.

Emson's will, dated April 25, 1895, named his daughter, Hannah, and Clifford Horner – listed as a friend – as the executors of his estate. The will left his wife their house with all of its furniture "that she desires" along with enough money to provide for all of her needs and that of their children, Christian and Hannah, for the remainder of their natural lives. The will was filed on June 23, 1896. His estate was estimated to be worth a half million dollars at the time of his death.

Hannah later married William L. Wilbur and moved to Stockton Street in Hightstown. Her brother, Christian, also lived on Stockton Street. In her later years, Sarah was in poor health and moved in with her daughter. Sarah died at the age of ninety on March 17, 1930 and was buried alongside her husband in the Cassville cemetery.

In Ephraim Emson's obituary and in some other references, mention is made of his benevolence. Dozens of mortgages held by him were exempt from the interest he could have rightfully claimed. Over two hundred people came to his funeral service.

After his death and the poverty of the Great Depression in the 1930's, many landowners fell delinquent in their taxes and their property was seized by Jackson Township.

With poverty engulfing the country, people turned to inexpensive or free means of entertainment to take their minds off their troubles. In the summer, this often meant taking the family to the nearest lake or beach to cool off and forget their woes for a few hours.

My parents and grandparents fondly remember "the ol' swimming hole." Those who lived in the time period between the Roaring 20's to President Kennedy's assassination, or know someone who did, will have their own coveted memories.

Setting out early on Saturday morning, stocking the car with enough food for an army, squeezing in the essentials like suntan lotion and plenty of towels, then piling the kids, neighbors, cousins and anyone else who would fit into the car and heading off for the nearest beach.

Beaches in those days bore little resemblance to the Seaside Heights and Wildwoods of today. There were no concession stands and lifeguard chairs. A beach was simply a stretch of sand alongside a lake or an ocean, surrounded by woods.

The adults would unload the car, spreading out the tablecloth and setting out the food while the children would change into their bathing suits and head for the water. The adults would eventually join the children in the water – splashing each other and jumping the waves – and periodically coming ashore to dry out and grab a sandwich.

Shuddering bodies with towels draped over their shoulders would gather at the water's edge, building sandcastles with receding moats or searching for fish in the shallow water's edge.

Residents of Jackson and New Egypt would drive to Oakford Lake in New Egypt or Colliers Mills Lake in Jackson. Families would head out after dinner, cooling off while swatting mosquitoes until it became too dark. Lazy summer weekends would be spent on the shores of those lakes.

An article in the April 29, 1934 edition of the Sunday Times mentions the town of New Egypt with its 1,200 residents swelling to more than 10,000 summer visitors occupying its twenty-five hotels and boarding houses.

Carolyn Lear, a New Egypt resident and member of its historical society, recalled how she and her brother would wait for their father to close up his shop promptly at six each evening. They would race into his car in their bathing suits and their mother would climb into the front and they would all head out to Colliers Mills Lake.

Lear recalls her father teaching her how to swim in that lake, and how many years later her husband taught their children to swim there as well. "There was no air conditioning in those days," Lear points out, "or even an electric fan so at the end of a hot day, you went down to the lake to cool off."

When people speak of Kennedy's assassination as "the end of Camelot" in a sense, it was. The idyllic time of innocence and freedom was forever lost. Over time, families moved apart, mothers returned to the workforce and distrust in government was met with increased regulations and restrictions.

But for one shining moment, life was filled with innocence….

Wildlife management areas were not created until the Pinelands National Reserve became our country's first reserve in 1978. As almost a premonition of what was to come, Stanley Switlik stated at the dedication of Lake Success, back in 1951:

"I am just a plain conservationist and I love this wilderness about us. It was my dream quite a few years ago that this Lake Success, which is about two hundred years old, should be rejuvenated and rebuilt…We have something very valuable in this part of New Jersey and I would suggest that we should get together and build a State Park that could commence at Colliers Mills to Toms River. Governor Driscoll stated in his remarks that New Jersey will be built up solid very soon from the Hudson to the Delaware. Now is the time we should save all of the possible open space for our children and grandchildren to play in the outdoors for the future…In closing, may the public, the hunters and fishermen always enjoy this place."

New Jersey Pine Barrens –
"The Last Great Place"

New Jersey is a land of contrasts. The fifth smallest state, it ranks ninth in population according to the 1990 census, making it the country's most densely populated state. Residents who reveal they are from New Jersey are often asked, "What exit?" – a reference to those who settled in towns located by exits off of the New Jersey Turnpike.

It is also a taunt by those who use the turnpike as a means to traverse the state to get to their final destinations outside of the state's borders. One of the principle reasons for its growth is the fact that it is centered between two major urban areas – New York and Philadelphia. Exploding growth is rampant throughout the state and developers are often at odds with conservationists.

New Jersey is known for its chemical and pharmaceutical industries, and as a byproduct, the state has the largest inventory of Superfund sites in the US.[15] Despite the heavy industry and intricate transportation system, the second largest industry is tourism and the

"Jersey Shore" is renowned for beckoning visitors to come relax by its surf and sand.

Technology is another major industry in the "Garden State". Major telecommunications and biotechnology firms make their home here less than an hour away from farmers toiling in their fields. The computer age has helped bring agriculture into the 21st century, yet many of the farmers are still using the tools of their forefathers while their offspring work for computer companies vying to build even better and faster microchips.

But the most unique contrast is this – despite burgeoning populations – New Jersey is home to the largest area of open space between Boston, Massachusetts and Richmond, Virginia.

This amazing ecosystem is referred to as the Pine Barrens, part of the Pinelands National Reserve. 1.1 million acres form the Pinelands National Reserve – an area federally designated in 1978. It encompasses parts of seven counties and includes fifty-six municipalities.

It is our country's first national reserve. United Nations Educational, Scientific and Cultural Organization (UNESCO) named it a Biosphere Reserve in 1983.[16] The Nature Conservancy has deemed it, "The Last Great Place."

The Pine Barrens envelop nearly a quarter of the state's landmass. Underneath its vast stretch, lies an aquifer containing almost 17 trillion gallons of some of the purest water on earth. This amount of water would cover the entire state ten feet deep.

What exactly is the Pine Barrens? It is believed to have originally gotten its name due to the belief that it was a stretch of dry, barren land. Nothing could be further from the truth. Almost forty animal species on the state's threatened and endangered list reside here. Among them are the Northern pine snake and barred owl.

There are plant species that exist here that are found nowhere else on earth, such as the bog asphodel. This striking member of the lily family grows in boggy areas. It blooms in late June, bursting forth with lacy yellow clusters of lily-like petaled flowers only four to nine millimeters in length.[17]

The bog asphodel once also existed in Delaware and the Carolinas, but is now extirpated from those states. There are less than 3,000 populations remaining today.

Fifty-four threatened and endangered plant species are protected under the Pinelands Comprehensive Management Plan. A complete list of these animal and plant species can be found in Appendix A.

Many plants and animal species reach their northern or southern range limits in the Pine Barrens. This is particularly evident in Colliers Mills, which is located in the northern end of the Pine Barrens. You can see the changeover in soils in several areas of Colliers Mills, from the rich, fertile farmland soil of the neighboring townships to the more common sandy soil found in the pinelands. Around the numerous cedar swamp bogs, the soil is predominantly acidic.

These wetland soils and surrounding vegetation help purify the aquifer by removing heavy metals and other contaminants. Vegetation such as sphagnum moss soaks up water in the surrounding beds and prevents runoff.

Sphagnum moss is a unique plant. It is able to absorb moisture up to five times its own weight. The secret lies in its intricate matrix of capillaries and surrounding air spaces, allowing water to be trapped and held like a sponge. Because of its absorption Native Americans used the moss for diapers. As far back as 1014, a Gaelic Chronicle indicates the moss was used for the dressing of wounds.[18] Germans used it as surgical dressing.[19]

Sphagnum not only absorbs water from the ground below, but can also leach it from the atmosphere, ensuring its survival during droughts. This amazing ability to collect and retain moisture may explain the abundance of orchid varieties found throughout the Pine Barrens, which are dependent on a constant source of moisture. Biologists have used the moss as a planting medium to grow orchids in the lab.

But sphagnum lined bogs are only part of the Pine Barrens mystique. The underlying land structure itself is part of the reason for its vast, pure aquifer. To understand this, we must look at how the Pine Barrens was formed.

New Jersey is home to five geographic ranges – Highlands, Valley and Ridge, Piedmont, Inner Coastal Plain, and Outer Coastal Plain. The latter are sometimes referred to as the Atlantic Coastal Plain.

Centuries ago, the Atlantic Ocean repeatedly washed over the Atlantic Coastal Plain and retreated, leaving sand and mineral deposits. When the ice age ended, glacial deposits formed hills while the receding ice carved numerous rivers and streams.

The cold air from the glaciers created temperatures twenty to thirty degrees lower than our present average. The sea level was much lower than today as well, because the melting glaciers still held vast amounts of water. Because of this, New Jersey's shoreline extended eighty miles east of where it ends today.

The low-lying areas of the Atlantic Coastal Plain were left with large amounts of sand and gravel on its surface. Vegetation began to grow from the mineral rich soil and animal populations moved in.

Along the northwestern fringes of Colliers Mills lies the Coastal Divide, or the area where the Inner and Outer Coastal Plains meet. Rivers and streams to the east of the Coastal Divide, such as the Toms River and Mullica River flow toward the Atlantic Ocean. Those west of the Divide, including Rancocas Creek, flow toward the Delaware River.

However, all the streams located within the Pine Barrens start as groundwater. No streams flow into the Pine Barrens from outside the region.[16] Underneath the Coastal Divide then, sits the headwaters of these vital waterways and is a convincing reason why this area needs protection. After all, the growing populations of Ocean, Burlington, and five other counties will draw some of their drinking water from sources that start here.

The Pine Barrens lie along the Outer Coastal Plain. It is made up of layers of sand, gravel and clay that are less than twenty feet thick along its western fringe but increase as they extend toward the Atlantic Ocean, becoming more than 1,000 feet thick at the Continental Shelf.[21]

The clay layers make up approximately twenty percent of this formation and are red, white, yellow or light gray in color. They act like giant filters, trapping and cleansing the water as it slowly drains through them. Each layer of clay may be as much as twenty-five feet thick.[22]

The Cohansey aquifer is the reservoir of water that lies near the surface in the Pine Barrens, feeding its many streams, creeks and bogs. Underneath that, lays the older Kirkwood aquifer that replenishes the water table.

These two aquifers supply the bulk of the private water systems of homeowners in and around the perimeter of the Pine Barrens. Even as early as 1876, some people realized the precious value of the water lying beneath the Pine Barrens.

Joseph Wharton, a Philadelphia financier, purchased 100,000 acres of pristine land around the defunct Batso iron smelter in the Pine Barrens, with the idea of exporting the water to his hometown. Lawmakers banned the move before Wharton had a chance to enact his plans and in 1981, the Legislature banned the export of water more than ten miles from the Pinelands National Reserve boundaries.[23]

From artifacts that have been unearthed and the use of carbon-14 dating, it is now known that the Paleo-Indians and not the Lenape, were the first Native Americans in this area. They were believed to have inhabited most of North America.

The Paleo-Indians hunted mammoth, elk, walrus and other mammals, killing them with crude projectiles. Skeletons of these mammals along with rudimentary arrowheads have been found in these areas.

The Pine Barrens do not consist only of pine trees, but also contain a substantial amount of Northern red oak, the state's official tree.

Along the bogs are stands of Atlantic white cedar, whose super straight trunks are used for utility poles. Its range is limited to swamps along the Atlantic Coastal Plain.

Numerous Eastern red cedar line the Pine Barrens as well, although these are not actually members of the cedar family, but belong to the cypress family. They are easily distinguished from the Atlantic white cedar by their reddish brown bark and twigs. The Eastern red cedar can tolerate bogs and wetlands but prefers poor, dry soil, making it highly adaptable to the Pine Barrens.

Pine trees, especially the pitch pine found in the pinelands, are quickly dwarfed in size by the rapidly growing red oaks. Even scrub oak, which makes up most of the undergrowth in Colliers Mills, can obtain heights of forty feet, overshadowing young pines.

Here is where an interesting adaptation of nature comes into play. Although all pines produce seed-bearing cones, that of the pitch pine is the one most easily recognized. The seeds inside the cone are held in place by a resin. This resin was used for torches by the early settlers and later for turpentine and rosin.

Unless scattered by animals, the resin must be melted by fire to release the seeds. Since pitch pines cannot stand overcrowding, fire serves another purpose – to kill off the surrounding trees and underbrush. The dark, thick-scaled bark of the pitch pine protects it from the heat of the fire.

In the newly cleared and charred ground, young trees will emerge from the seeds, often within weeks of the blaze. Needles of the mature trees will first re-sprout from the bark, then from along the branches.

As if planned by nature, periodic fires will spread through the Pine Barrens, reshaping the forestry scene. Because most of the Pine Barrens is privately held, firefighters will employ "control" or "prescribed" burning to create artificial firebreaks to protect homes from fire outbreaks.

Ocean County, because of its sandy soils with loamy surfaces, is more susceptible to fires than the southern end of the Pinelands where the clay soil holds in moisture.

Campfires and carelessly thrown matches are always a concern during dry, windy days. In 1995, a fire started this way that burned over 19,200 acres. This is only one of many notable fires that destroyed large amounts of acreage.

Fire towers are scattered throughout the Pine Barrens and manned twenty-four hours a day throughout the fire season. From their height, fires can be spotted before spreading too far.

One fire tower, in particular, located on Apple Pie Hill in the Wharton State Forest preserve, reaches two hundred-five feet into the air to provide spectacular views of the Pine Barrens. On a clear day, visibility stretches from the Atlantic Ocean to the skyline of Philadelphia, providing a complete east-to-west view of the state.

From its fire-adaptive techniques to its seemingly endless water supply, the Pine Barrens is a unique area to behold. Exploring the trails of Colliers Mills is a great way to grasp a portion of the ecological significance of this magnificent stretch of land. For those who will not have the chance to experience this area in person, follow along as we step past the pines...

Flights of Fancy

Turkeys are amazingly smart birds. I watched in fascination one day as a family of wild turkeys crossed our street. One of the adults stood by one side of the road, while another adult waited on the destination side as the babies crossed. This in itself is contrary to most birds that scramble across the road haphazardly. But here is the incredible part – a third adult planted itself in the middle of the road, making sure all the babies got across in a line – its behavior reminiscent of a school crossing guard.

Another time, I saw a flock of turkeys quickly darting across a grassy embankment alongside a road. When they reached the road, they all came to an abrupt halt. Traffic was fairly heavy, so instead of crossing on foot as they usually do, they all lifted off and flew across the road. When they reached the other side, they landed and continued across the field.

I remember the year that flocks of turkeys appeared on our wooded property. It was the first time I had seen wild turkeys up close and personal. I wondered why so many of them had suddenly appeared, when I hadn't seen any in previous years.

During a Boy Scout hike through Colliers Mills, the Fish and Wildlife Conservation Officer leading the tour mentioned that wild turkeys had recently been reintroduced to Colliers Mills for hunting purposes. Despite the large number brought into the park, the hunters were unable to find any. That explained the impromptu visit to my property, where hunting is banned.

Wild turkeys have been successfully reintroduced into all areas of New Jersey through the Division of Fish and Wildlife's restoration program. The program was launched in 1978 when biologists from the division introduced fifteen gobblers and seven hens from New York and Vermont to Sussex County. The birds were carefully watched and monitored over the next few years and as the birds began successfully breeding, more were introduced in other parts of the state.

During the trap and transfer program — a program that traps turkeys in areas that are plentiful and transfers them to areas of low or non-existent population — seventy-seven birds from Alabama, Arkansas, Georgia and South Carolina were also introduced in the hope that the wild turkey would gain a foothold in similar ecosystems.

One thousand three hundred seventy-eight turkeys were transferred during the program, with Ocean County receiving the most at two hundred sixty-five birds. Trapping the turkeys is difficult as the birds have exceedingly sharp reflexes and keen eyesight for movement. Their hearing is also several times greater than that of humans.

Only half the birds that are lured out with corn are caught with the division's rocket nets at any given time. Originally, Cannon Net Devices were used which contained loosely fitting weighted shells and explosives that when detonated, fired the nets over the wildlife. Today, rocket nets are used. These work like a non-aerodynamic rocket because the entire chamber containing the explosive is lofted by the charge detonation. The rockets — or recoilless cannons, as they are sometimes called — contain a blunt nosecone, a hollow body tube, exhaust ports and a stabilizing fin. The rockets are connected to the nets with a rope.[24]

With its wingspan of five feet, the wild turkey is the largest bird in the forest. Benjamin Franklin wanted the turkey for our national bird, but it lost by one congressional vote. In his letter to his daughter, Sarah, Franklin claimed:

"I wish that the bald eagle had not been chosen as the representative of our country, he is a bird of bad moral character, he does not get his living honestly, you may have seen him perched on some dead tree, where, too lazy to fish for himself, he watches the labor of the fishing-hawk, and when that diligent bird has at length taken a fish, and is bearing it to its nest for the support of his mate and young ones, the bald eagle pursues him and takes it from him.... Besides he is a rank coward; the little kingbird, not bigger than a sparrow attacks him boldly and drives him out of the district. He is therefore by no means a proper emblem for the brave and honest. .. of America.... For a truth, the turkey is in comparison a much more respectable bird, and withal a true original native of America ... a bird of courage, and would not hesitate to attack a grenadier of the British guards, who should presume to invade his farmyard with a red coat on."[25]

As with most birds, the male – called a tom — is larger and more colorful. They are also the only bird that has a beard. This "beard" is actually a series of long hair like feathers. The average turkey has between 5,000 and 7,000 feathers on its entire body.

Toms can weigh between sixteen and twenty-four pounds. The female, or hen as she is called, is much smaller at eight to ten pounds. The hen's drab brownish color helps camouflage her and her offspring, which are called poults. Poults begin eating seeds, nuts and berries within twelve to twenty-four hours of birth. Adults will add acorns, insects and small reptiles to their diets.

Turkeys have a wide range of vocalizations from a clicking sound to a purr that sounds like a contented cat going to sleep, to a "bark" that you could mistake for a small dog. And of course, there is the gobble sound that we are all familiar with.

Turkeys can also run up to twenty-five miles per hour and fly at thirty-five miles per hour. It's hard to believe that such an adept bird almost became extinct in the 1930's, but thanks to reintroduction methods, there are almost 6.4 million wild turkeys in the world today.[26]

The mockingbird (*Mimus polyglottos*) is a very interesting bird. In the movie, "To Kill a Mockingbird", the character Miss Maudie explains that "it's a sin to kill a mockingbird" because "Mockingbirds don't do one thing but make music for us to enjoy. They don't eat up peoples' gardens, don't nest in corncribs, they don't do one thing but sing their hearts out for us."

While not dangerous, mockingbirds are fiercely territorial and the male will valiantly defend its nest while babies are present. When defending their nest, they will just as easily take on a human as another bird or animal. It has been noted that mockingbirds can actually distinguish between different people.[27]

This exceptional memory aids them in song. Mockingbirds are

experts at accurately mimicking sounds around them – other birds, animals, humans and even machinery! Two males in Florida were found to have vocabularies of almost two hundred calls each. They will sing in flight as well as when perched.

They are also quite chatty at night. Most birds do not make sounds after dark, so if you have mockingbirds in the area and hear lots of "bird chatter" during the night, mockingbirds are the likely culprits.

Mockingbirds are most easily distinguished by sight. These gray and white birds, about nine inches in length, have white patches under the wing, which are quite visible in flight. Their tails stick up in an awkward manner. Mockingbirds will often flick their tails in a deliberate manner when perched.

They prefer short grass and weeds and will usually be found in areas of open, cut fields and on lawns neighboring the wildlife management area.

The catbird (*Dumetella carolinensis*) is the only bird with a solid dark gray body. The underside of its tail is a rusty color and it has a black cap on its head. It is about eight inches long.

The catbird will probably greet you when you first enter Colliers Mills. He has appointed himself the unofficial mascot of the woods, greeting newcomers and warning other birds of their presence. The catbird is exceedingly curious and will usually follow you along on your travels, hopping from branch to branch to get a closer look.

Catbirds can also mimic the calls of other birds, but don't do it nearly as well as the mockingbird. They are found in almost all of the fifty states and south into Central America. They prefer pines and underbrush, but also live among maples, oak and birch. They prefer unscorched areas and frequent prescribed burning will decrease their population.

The pine siskin (*Carduelis pinus*) is quite the acrobat, balancing upside down from a branch to pluck seeds from a cone or seedpod. They prefer the seeds of birches, alders, cedars and hemlock trees. They also have a fondness for salt and may be seen alongside snow-plowed roads that have been recently salted.[28]

Pine siskins are members of the finch family and fly in the undulating flight pattern distinctive of finches. Their dark streaked body ranges from four and a half to five inches in length and they have a yellow patch on their wings and tail. Their beaks are short and cone-shaped. Typically, pine siskins travel in flocks.

The Yellow-throated warbler (*Dendroica dominica*) is common in Colliers Mills, although not easily seen. It tends to stay high in the trees and prefers mixed forests that are predominantly pine. It has a yellow throat, white belly and black and white head with black streaks across its breast. Its most identifying feature is a white band above its eye. This warbler lives mainly in the southeastern part of the United States and reaches the end of its northern range in New Jersey.

There are two hundred-fourteen species of woodpeckers. Their tapping sounds echoes through the woods of Colliers Mills as they peck at trees for wood-boring insects. Woodpeckers have very long tongues, to enable them to reach insects inside the holes they have drilled. They also have special "shock absorbing" muscles in their head that protect them as they drill.

The red-headed woodpecker (*Melanerpes erythrocephalus*) is a threatened species in several states in the US, including New Jersey. Those unfamiliar with woodpeckers may confuse this species with the common red-bellied woodpecker (*Centurus Carolinus*) or Pileated woodpecker *(Dryocopus pileatus)*, although the markings are very different.

The red-headed woodpecker, true to its name, has a red head with a white breast and black wings with a wide white stripe, making it look like it is wearing a tuxedo.

The red-bellied woodpecker (*Melanerpes carolinus*) on the other hand, has only a red cap with a white face and breast. Its wings have many smaller stripes of black and white.

The Pileated woodpecker (*Dryocopus pileatus*) has a solid black back and wing with a black stripe across its white face. The top of its head is red and pointed, unlike the two previously mentioned woodpeckers, whose heads are rounded.

The population of red-headed woodpeckers has declined due to habitat destruction, past hunting of the species for its beautiful plumage and a decline in its food sources. Colliers Mills is an ideal location for this bird, as it prefers open grassland, open deciduous and riparian woodlands and flooded bottomland forests.

It has a varied diet of nuts, fruit, seeds, insects, bird eggs, mice and even smaller adult birds. Out of all the woodpecker species, the red-headed woodpecker is most adept at fly catching. It will store its food in tree cavities and is the only woodpecker that will cover its food stash with tree bark or other material.

Hummingbirds produce the world's tiniest egg. The ruby throated hummingbird (*Archilochus colubris*) is the only hummingbird species in the northeast. Often called hummers by bird fanciers, they are known for their agility and wing speed. The ruby throated hummingbird's wings beat an average of fifty times per second, producing the humming sound which gives them their common name.

Hummers drink nectar from tubular flowers such as salvia, bee balm, petunia and trumpet creeper. They are particularly attracted to the color red and will readily accept sugar water from feeders. Since hummers are constantly in motion, never hovering for more than a minute, their energy needs are great. Hummers will consume up to two-thirds of their body weight in food per day.

They are the only birds that can fly backward equally as well as forward. They move their wings in a figure - eight motion versus the back and forward wing motion of most birds.

Hummers are fiercely territorial. The males will weave and bob in flight with each other, over property disputes, reminiscent of a boxing match. While sparring, they will emit a mouse-like squeaking sound.

Turkey vultures (*Cathartes aura*) are a very common sight in this area, particularly in Colliers Mills. They are attracted to the smell of decaying carrion. Engineers have found this skill to be useful as leaking fuel pipes produce a similar smell. By following clustering vultures, engineers have been able to detect leaking underground fuel pipes.

Dying animals will usually attempt to crawl into the woods to avoid predators and deer are no exception. Whether wounded by hunters or hit by cars, they provide a steady meal for the vultures. By feeding on dead animals, vultures serve a useful purpose by preventing the spread of disease that would result from the rotting corpses and maggots.

Vultures generally fly in groups, with one slightly ahead of the others as they glide in widening circles, surveying the ground below. Turkey vultures are very similar in appearance to black vultures, which are also found in this area.

Black vultures are solid in color. When in flight, the lighter colored wingtips of the turkey vulture help to distinguish it from the black vulture.

Turkey vultures belong to a family that includes condors. They are roughly the size of an eagle, with wingtips stretching six feet wide. At night they will roost, typically in the lower branches of trees or occasionally on rooftops. Many is the morning that I've come out for my morning paper and felt eyes upon me only to turn around and see several turkey vultures camped out on my roof.

The Cooper's hawk (*Accipiter cooperii*) is one of three North American hawks that prey on birds. It is listed as a threatened species on the state list. Until 1999, it was classified as endangered but its population is increasing. The Cooper's hawk has been seen in the vicinity of Colliers Mills.

Preferred breeding areas include mixed, deciduous or coniferous forests with dense canopies near clearing or open habitats.[29] Cooper's hawks make a distinctive nest, mainly out of twigs, with a "bump-out" so it can sit comfortably in the nest with its tail sticking out over the bump.

This hawk is about the size of a crow, with short, rounded wings and a long, narrow tail. The tail is rounded with a white tip on the edges of its feathers. In flight, its silhouette appears cross-shaped with dark brown and white striped wings. A fast flyer, Cooper's hawks cut through the air with strong, powerful wing beats.

The Cooper's hawk does not bite its prey to kill it like falcons do; instead it will hold it away from its body and squeeze it repeatedly until it dies. On occasion, it will hold its prey under water until it drowns.[30]

I saw my first great blue heron (*Butorides striatus*) perched in the branches of a dead tree, on the outskirts of Colliers Mills. He sat, watching, as if he were the park's patriarch. The tree he chose overlooked a wetlands area and provided him a vantage point to see frogs moving about in the sphagnum moss.

Frogs and fish are the heron's main diet, although it will also feed upon small mammals, reptiles and even other birds. Herons generally migrate south in the fall; those that don't may perish if the winter is particularly harsh and they are unable to find food.

The great blue heron is a lanky bird with a height of thirty-nine to fifty-two inches and long greenish-yellow legs. Its feathers are mostly gray, with some black and white markings around the head, bend of wing and underside. Its cry is a hoarse, guttural squawk as it takes to flight. It flies with its neck folded – a telltale sign of this species.

The bald eagle (*Haliaeetus leucocephalus*) is known to most of us either through pictures or from the back of a dollar bill. It became our National Emblem on June 20, 1782 when the Great Seal of the United States was adopted.

This majestic symbol of the United States is facing declining population. While the eagle was removed from the threatened species list in 2004, it remains under the federal Bald Eagle Protection Act of 1940, which "prohibits the take, transport, sale, barter, trade, import and export, and possession of eagles, making it illegal for anyone to collect eagles and eagle parts, nests, or eggs without a permit."[31]

The bald eagle feeds mainly upon dead fish washed up on beaches and riverfronts.[32] These fish are often laden with pesticides — one reason for the eagle's reduced numbers. Loss of habitat, hunting and poaching have also contributed to their diminishing numbers.

Its height averages thirty-one inches, but it has a wingspread of seventy-two to ninety inches. It is mainly black in color, with a white head and a long yellow beak.

There have been bald eagle sightings at Colliers Mills, but I haven't been lucky enough yet to catch a glimpse of this magnificent bird in the wild.

The Canada goose (*Branta Canadensis*) is a migratory bird that is rapidly becoming semi-domesticated and no longer inclined to migrate. Their spreading population has become troublesome to towns where they have taken up residence in local parks, golf courses and even large lawns.

They vary in size from twenty-two inches – around the size of a mallard duck – all the way up to forty-five inches. Mainly brown in color with a recognizable black head and neck they have a large white patch on each check.

When danger approaches, they will pull their wings slightly out to the sides and back and extend their necks parallel to the ground. By making themselves lower to the ground, they become less visible to predators. This also gives a threatening appearance to those who do see them. If the first warning is not heeded, the goose will continue to advance and issue another warning by hissing.

Their familiar honking fills the air around Colliers Mills Lake, one of many local bodies of water that they like to frequent.

I watched them one night as they skimmed across the surface of the lake, just as the sun began to set. At first, they were scattered across the glassy surface of the lake. Then a few of them began to honk and lift out of the water, flapping their wings. This was a signal to the others who began moving closer together until the large mass of geese had been split into small groups.

Others tossed their heads from side to side. The reason for this behavior is to shake off any mud or excess water before flight. One goose in the group began honking and flapping his wings again. Others began to imitate him and soon they were all doing it in this one little group. In synchronized rhythm, they lifted off and rapidly formed their familiar "V" shape. Then the next group began and so on, until there were several Vs skimming the surface of the clouds. I watched their reflection in the water until they became dots on the horizon.

It's scenes like this that convince me of the intelligence among all living creatures. The exodusI had just witnessed had not been choreographed by instinct alone, but through carefully rehearsed communication.

The reason that geese and ducks fly in a V-shaped pattern is to conserve energy. The currents generated by each bird in the formation help propel the next bird's motion. They also trade places in the formation that helps them fly greater distances.

The barred owl (*Strix varia*) takes its name from the brown striping across its neck, breast and belly. Its other feathers are gray. Barred owls are large and stocky.

Owls in colder regions have more plumage than owls in warm climates, giving them a plumper appearance. They often have thick feathers covering their legs as well for additional warmth. This also serves to protect them from bites as they carry their prey back to the nest.

Barred owls prefer wetlands and swamp forests. Owls are nocturnal, relying on their keen sense of hearing to track prey. Barred owls rest in thick tree groves during the day and feed at night upon a diet of birds, rodents, frogs and crayfish.

Many people think that owls rely on their eyesight, but it is really their hearing that aids them in hunting. An owl's eyes occupy more than half of its head and cannot move inside its sockets. So owls must turn their head to see peripherally. To enable them to do this, they have fourteen vertebrae in their necks, whereas giraffes and humans only have seven. This allows them to turn their heads slightly more than one hundred and eighty degrees.

Their beaks are situated lower on the head than most birds, so that it doesn't block their vision. They can see very well in low light conditions due to a reflective layer behind the retina called a tapetum. Cats also have a tapetum, which gives their eyes that yellowish glow in the dark. It is unknown whether owls can see color and even if they did, it would be of little benefit since they hunt in darkened conditions.

Owls actually have three eyelids. They use one for cleaning the eye, one for blinking and the other for sleeping.[33] By closing one of their eyelids, they can protect their eye from pieces of food while they are chewing and still be able to see.

The colored part of the eye, called the iris, indicates when the owl will feed. Those with yellowish irises hunt during the day, those with orange, at dusk and dark-eyed owls hunt at night. Irises also control the size of the pupil. Owls are the only birds whose pupils can contract and dilate independently of each other. This is helpful if the owl is sitting in filtered shade with one eye in direct sunlight while the other is shaded.

All owls lay white eggs.[34] The eggs are laid over a period of several days. This allows the offspring to fledge (leave the nest) independently and provides a better chance for survival.

Barred owls are identified by their call. It sounds like the question, "Who cooks for you?" with the last note slighter higher than the rest. Seen in the vicinity of Colliers Mills, the barred owl is considered a threatened species in the state of New Jersey.

Brown-headed cowbirds are very common in Colliers Mills. They are often mistaken for starlings, grackles and blackbirds, all which will mingle with the cowbird. They have short, cone-shaped bills, pointy wings and rounded tails. The males have brown heads and shiny greenish-black bodies, their feathers are iridescent. The females are more of a brownish-gray color, with a slight greenish sheen. The eyes, legs and beaks of both genders are black.

Cowbirds do not build their own nests. They place their eggs in the nest of another unsuspecting bird, which incubates them as her own. They will lay as many as forty eggs during the year and over one hundred bird species have played surrogate mother to them. The most commonly used nests belong to yellow warblers, Eastern towhees, red-winged blackbirds and various sparrows.

The female will lay an egg in a nest whose eggs are typically smaller than her own. This interesting pattern was born of practicality. Cowbirds feed on insects attracted to cattle and horses. You may have seen birds "riding" on the backs of horses. They are actually picking ticks and other bugs off of the horse's back.

Back in the days when bison roamed this country, cowbirds would follow the herds. Unable to care for their young in a stationery nest while they traveled with the bison, cowbirds began leaving their eggs in other bird's nests so they could be raised and continue the species.

Even though the herds of bison are gone, to this day, cowbirds continue to take advantage of the unsolicited hospitality of other birds.

Why don't the mothers evict these uninvited guests? Usually, they don't recognize the eggs or offspring as not being theirs until they have become too large for the host bird to remove.

Those mothers who do catch the "guest egg" in time may cover it with nesting material to insulate it from being incubated and hatched. Yellow warbler nests have been found to have as many as six layers between the eggs.

I am always in awe of the bird watcher who can walk into a forest amid the banter of a dozen birds or so and pick out individual birds by their calls.

How do you learn to identify individual species in the middle of a forest? Well, there are a few things to consider. When you first step into a forest, especially if you have not attempted to be as quiet as possible, the birds will scatter. There are a few keys things to remember.

First, you are on "their turf," so as a visitor, you need to be as quiet and unobtrusive as possible. Second, birds are skitterish by nature. They survive by being alert and aware of their surroundings.

Then there's time spent grooming themselves to keep their feathers in tiptop shape for flight, searching for a mate, building a nest or feeding their young. They don't have time to wait for you to leave so they can resume their chores, so they will move to another area to work until you have left.

If they have chicks that they are feeding, they don't want you to know where the nest is, so they will not enter or approach it while you are there unless absolutely necessary. In settings such as your backyard where you come in close constant contact with birds, they will condition themselves to your presence over time.

Some birds, like animals, become accustomed to people and their habits. They know that you fill the feeders at ten o'clock or make frequent trips to the clothesline. Despite this, they would still prefer not having you there – or at least knowing you are there. There are exceptions of course, particularly with urban birds, such as pigeons, that know most of their meals are handouts from people.

Waterfowl like ducks and Canada Geese have also gotten used to handouts and may brazeningly walk up to you looking for food.

They may even snatch food from the hand of a child. The feeding of waterfowl at public parks has resulted in flocks of Canada Geese who no longer migrate. These "resident geese" have been conditioned to being fed by people year round and this has contributed to larger flocks, unacceptable levels of coliform in the water from their droppings and even attacks on people.

I was on the boardwalk in Wildwood a few years ago when two seagulls flew over the entrance of a pizzeria as someone was exiting with a slice. The birds turned and swooped down, scaring the person who screamed and dropped her pizza. The birds quickly snatched it up. I thought this was an isolated incident until I saw them approach the next person leaving the pizzeria with food in hand. This time, their cries and low flying caused the person to drop the pizza immediately. Again, they flew down and grabbed their meal. When the performance was repeated a third time, I knew the birds had conditioned themselves to getting meals this way.

Birds, like animals, are highly adaptive. Unfortunately, this learned behavior is not always in their best interests. Disturbing habitats, razing land for developments, introducing foreign birds to our shores and eliminating predators all upset the balance of nature.

So, the next time you're walking in the woods, step lightly. Try to be as unobtrusive as possible. Do not toss food meant for human consumption to the birds. Let them fly about their tasks as nature intended. The best way to observe birds is to sit quietly without making a sound and let the birds resume their routine. Any movement of your body will catch their eye and frighten them.

Professional photographers often use a bird blind – a manmade partition placed in a strategic area and left in place. It is often painted to blend in with the surroundings. Over time, birds get used to its presence and since there is no movement, they are not disturbed by it. The photographer can stand behind the blind and shoot pictures through a hole cut in the blind, unnoticed by the birds.

But you do not need anything this fancy and in fact, permanent blinds are prohibited in most wildlife management areas, such as

Colliers Mills. Instead, just lean back, get comfortable and sit quietly without moving for at least twenty minutes. Gradually, you will notice birds chirping and hopping from branch to branch. Watch the sky overhead for falcons, vultures and hawks. The best times to observe are early morning as the sun starts to climb and just before dusk.

Visit different habitats and return at different times of the day. You might see waterfowl at Colliers Mills Lake early in the morning and encounter songbirds in the woods around mid-morning. Certain types of birds prefer open fields, other prefer marshy swamps.

When you become more versed with bird watching and learn the diets of various birds, you will be able to seek out habitats that are plentiful in that food. Goldfinches are thistle eaters, while hummingbirds seek the nectar from trumpet shaped flowers. Some birds may be insect eaters; others prefer grain or seed and still others, berries and fruit.

How do you identify which birds you are seeing? I started out by purchasing a good pair of binoculars and a pocket field guide of birds in my area. There are several well-established guides out there, by authors such as Peterson and Stokes.[35]

I then started with birds I could identify accurately, for example – robins and blue jays. I looked up their average size in my field guide (robins are eight and a half inches, blue jays are ten inches). Then I made a mental picture of these birds to use this as a guide when viewing unknown birds.

If the unidentified bird you're looking at is close to the size of a robin and is red, look up red birds around eight and a half inches long. Most guides divide birds by color and body type. Measurements are usually given alongside the picture to make identification faster.

As I got better at judging sizes and noting colorations before the birds flew off, I began working on other characteristics. Besides the body color, what color is the underside? Wings? Top of the head? Is there a circle or bar around the eye? What about a patch of color on the wings when extended in flight?

What about the beak – is it short and stout, or long and thin? Is it straight or hooked? What color is it?

Is the tail long and slender? Rounded or pointed? Does it stick up like a mockingbird's tail?

If the bird is in flight, does it glide on air currents? Beat its wings forcefully? Does it fly in a straight line or in an undulating (wave) pattern, which is indicative of finches?

These are just the visible clues. Calls are important and even if you can't identify them at first, practice discerning them from each other. Sometimes the chatter can get so loud that it seems as if all the birds are talking at once. Baby birds tend to have weak, pleading cries that are intermittent. Other birds have warning cries or might sound off as they disembark from a branch.

Keep in mind the time of the year as well. Are birds starting to migrate? In Colliers Mills, you might see birds not found in this area passing through in the fall on their way south. If you are lucky, you might have an "accidental sighting" of a bird out of his range that has wandered off course.

If it is spring or early summer, you may see immature birds whose color markings may be lighter or not fully developed. Males of the species will typically be brighter colored and marked; females may be a dull gray or brown.

After you have done this for a while, you will start getting used to a familiar pattern. You'll catch the up and down movement of a finch out of the corner of your eye and recognize it. If you have a hummingbird feeder, you'll learn to recognize the chirping sounds of males fighting over territory. Crows have a very distinctive "caw-caw-caw" sound that you will never forget.

Before long, there will be dozens of birds in your mental inventory. You'll become adept at recognizing their size, wing coloration or beak shape. If bird watching is a hobby you enjoy, you might consider looking for a local group to join. Watching and listening to experienced birders will help you gain knowledge as to what to look for, as well as tips on a particular species.

Colliers Mills, with its varied habitats, has a lot to offer a birder. In fact, it is often used in bird counts – organized events by groups like the Audubon Society to measure the population of species. Without input from individuals, it would be hard for organizations to track changes, such as a decline in a particular species. There are eight hundred different bird species in the United States, according to the Audubon Society.

Birds can provide hours of relaxing entertainment as we watch them feeding their young, amusing us with their antics or battling over territory. They are amazing creatures that have become highly adaptive.

The average bird's heartbeat is four hundred beats per minute while resting and up to 1,000 beats per minute when in flight. Birds are unable to sweat and their average body temperature is about seven to eight degrees higher than that of a human. Up to three-quarters of the air they draw in is used to cool their bodies.

> *"Hey farmer, farmer, put away your DDT*
> *I don't care about spots on my apples,*
> *Leave me the birds and the bees, please"*[36]

When Joni Mitchell sang these lyrics from *"Big Yellow Taxi"* – which was released in 1970 debate over the widespread use of DDT was still raging.

Dichloro-diphenyl-trichloroethane (DDT) was patented in the United States in 1943. It was actually created in 1874, but it wasn't until 1939 that Dr. Paul Muller discovered its effectiveness as a pesticide.[37] In 1948, he won the Nobel Prize for his work with DDT.

It quickly became one of the world's most widely used pesticides, wiping out millions of flies, mosquitoes and lice. Drug manufacturer Merck produced it to help squelch a growing epidemic of typhus. Farmers used it on their crops. The U.S. Army used it to kill lice on soldiers.

DDT quickly found its way into the water supply, where fish absorbed it. The chemical built up in plants and the fatty tissues of birds and animals. It was blamed for the decline of bird species that ate fish contaminated with DDT.

It was believed these birds produced thinner shelled eggs whose chicks did not always survive. However, proponents of the pesticide point to studies showing some of these species' populations actually increased during the time period that DDT was on the market and that other factors contributed to declines where they existed.

Regardless, it was banned in the US in 1972 after a three year examination of the pesticide. William D. Ruckelshaus, Administrator of the Environmental Protection at that time, declared, "that the continued massive use of DDT posed unacceptable risks to the environment and potential harm to human health."[38]

However, many countries around the world today continue to use it. It takes more than fifteen years to break down in our environment. We know now that it can cause damage to the liver, reproductive and nervous systems, and cause liver cancer.[39]

DDT is an example of a success story that became a nightmare. DDT killed malaria infected mosquitoes and is credited with saving over a half-million lives that would have been lost to this disease.

In the United States alone, approximately 675,000 tons of DDT was applied during its time on the market.[40] Its detrimental effects on wildlife were never conclusively proven and the battle continues to rage on both sides.

However, it is hard to believe that anything so toxic to insect life would not ultimately have some effect on the rest of life on this planet. Toward the end of its run in the US market, mosquitoes were rapidly learning to avoid the pesticide and those exposed started developing a resistance.[41] The extent of damage it would have caused, had it stayed on the market, will never be known, but nature was rapidly working to overcome this perceived threat.

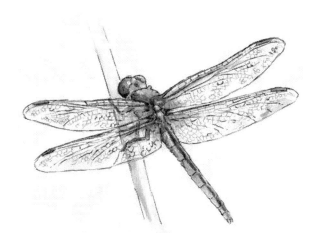

Ode to the Dragonfly

A graceful pixie, its lacy wings glistening in the morning sun, stops to rest nearby. It hesitates but a moment, then alights and flies off. It joins other delicate pixies as they play a random game of tag in the air.

Each one pauses for only a moment, resting on vegetation that lines the stream. You can observe the perfectly shaped wings as they stretch outward, nearly transparent with a touch of color along the top.

Its slender body juts into the air, like the final stroke of an artist's paintbrush before it leaves the canvas. The rounded head, with its bulging eyes, appears to study its surroundings. Then it pushes off and returns to flight.

These gentle fairies of flight pose no harm to the humans. Their voracious appetite is directed toward those smaller than them. They neither sting nor bite, although they can give you a harmless nip if handled.

Dragonflies belong to a scientific order known as Odonata. The word "odon" comes from the Greek and means "tooth". They use their sharp teeth to dissect other members of the insect class, mainly mosquitoes and flies.

Odonata, or "odes," as they are affectionately known by some who study them will feed upon whatever prey is available. Large dragonflies have even been known to eat smaller members of their species.

The females have an almost insatiable appetite when forming their eggs. Shortage of food sources can adversely affect reproductive behavior. The males are territorial and will protect their food sources for hours at a clip.

Over 5,000 species make up the order worldwide. There are four hundred and fifty species in North America. Odonates are divided into three living suborders: Anisoptera (which includes dragonflies), Zygoptera (which includes damselflies) and Anisozygoptera (which contains only two species found in Japan and the Himalayas).

Two other groups – Protodonata and Protoanisoptera – are extinct. The first group was discovered through fossils in sediment formed in Europe about three hundred and twenty-five million years ago. Protodonates' wingspan was up to thirty inches and they became extinct around the time dinosaurs appeared. Fossils of the latter group were found in limestone near Abilene, Kansas. Others were found in France. Protoanisopterans were also much larger than modern dragonflies.

Odonates are found on every continent except Antarctica. The majority of today's species live in tropical climates. Only the suborder Anisozygoptera is rarely seen and scientists have studied it mainly through fossils.

Females lay eggs in or near the water. They will spend the majority of their lives underwater as larvae, known as nymphs or naiads. This period can last from an average of one to two years to as long as six years, depending on the latitude and altitude in which they reside.

Nymphs have gills in the rectum through which they suck water and extract oxygen then expel the water violently, making their movements jet-propelled.

Nymphs will shed their skin — a process called molting —from six to fifteen times. In the last molt, they will leave the water and shed their gills along with their skin. Their wings are immediately functional, unlike beetles and butterflies that pass through a transitional stage in which their wings form and grow.

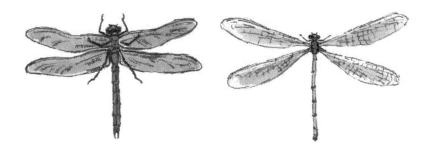

A dragonfly is seen on the left, a damselfly is on the right.

What is the difference between a dragonfly and a damselfly? Dragonflies are much larger, with thicker bodies. Their large compound eyes appear to be touching on some species. Dragonflies are considered to have the best eyesight of all insects that help them hunt and capture prey in flight.

Dragonflies have two pairs of wings; the top two wings and wing muscles are much larger, making it the stronger flier of the two. The wings of a damselfly are the same size and have a hinge, which allows them to fold them vertically when resting. This is the easiest way for the novice observer to identify the two groups – whether the wings are in an open or closed position when perching.

Damselflies are also more delicate, with slender bodies and smaller heads whose eyes do not appear to touch. They will hunt all year round, while dragonflies only look for prey in warmer weather.

Another key difference is that dragonflies mate in flight, with the male appearing to "hold" the female up into the air. Their copulation lasts from a few seconds to several minutes.

Damselflies will mate while perched or when flying to another perch. Their union will last from five to ten minutes. The males are fiercely competitive, especially during reproduction. The male of some species will actually remove sperm placed by other males from the female's body before mating!

Odonates are amazingly beautiful to watch in flight. Their speed and agility help them avoid a long list of predators, including birds, fish, spiders, lizards and frogs. Dragonflies can fly forward at approximately one hundred body-lengths per second and backward at three body-lengths per second. They can hover for about a minute in the air.

Odonates are held in high esteem by some cultures. In Japan they frequently appear in artwork. Other cultures fear or loathe them, bestowing such names as the "devil's darning needle" upon them.

They are always a welcome sight to the environmentalist. Odonates are believed to be bellwethers for a good ecosystem. If a biologist finds a number of these flitting about a lake, he knows the water is probably healthy. Different species prefer certain flora and environmental conditions. Having a large variety of species present usually indicates a diverse habitat of multiple ecological factors, dependent upon a healthy ecosystem.

Changes in water flow, force or pH can affect the vegetation that line its banks. Certain insects will only feed upon specific vegetation, such as the monarch butterfly that feeds upon milkweed. When these plants die off from a particular area, the insects that rely on them will move to another area as well. This in turn, affects species such as the dragonfly that feeds on the primary insects and so on up the food chain.

Numerous species of dragonfly and damselfly can be found in Colliers Mills. It is even home to two state endangered species that I uncovered one summer while studying them. One of them is the golden-winged skimmer (*Libellula auripennis*) – a beautiful dragonfly that looks as if its lacy wings were dipped in fluorescent orange paint. Its body has a shiny, almost iridescent golden orange glow to it.

Its unusual coloring caught my eye while I was photographing other odonates. Unlike the others, it was the only one of its species that I saw. It mingled with the others and at first I thought perhaps it was a color variant. When it stopped for a moment to rest on a twig nearby, I could see its distinct differences.

As if posing for its picture, it alit just long enough for me to depress the shutter, and then disappeared from my sight, as if it had been an illusion. I never saw the golden winged skimmer again, but I am glad that it delighted me with its presence that day.

There are numerous bar winged skimmers (*Libellula axilena*) – the other endangered species that I identified – in Colliers Mills. This dragonfly has clearly marked features unlike any others. Its bright blue body is more slender than the other skimmers. Its oversized head is purplish in color, giving the appearance of an overripe grape. The wings have a black edging at the top and end of each wing.

I found the bar winged skimmers along the edge of a lake, along a stream and even resting on some vegetation alongside the water's edge. I was surprised to find out that they were endangered, as Colliers Mills appears to have a healthy population of them.

What I found interesting in identifying the odonates was how closely they matched the pictures in the guides – unlike the trees, salamanders and others that I tried to match up – the odonates never seemed to vary off the standard model. It was heartening to find something easy to identify for a beginner. Of course, the real challenge was being patient enough for them to grow weary of their "air dancing" and rest for a moment – just long enough to observe their features.

Although this chapter focuses on odonates, I'd like to spend some time talking about a less welcome visitor found in Colliers Mills. While there are many beautiful and beneficial members of the animal kingdom to behold, there are also some that can pose harm to the hiker.

By now, Lyme disease has practically become a household word, especially in this area. Lyme disease was named for the town in which it was first identified – Lyme, Connecticut. It quickly spread throughout the northeast and has now been documented in at least forty-six states.

A significant number of people in the Colliers Mills area are victims of this disease which is spread by ticks — a member of the arachnid family — but that should not prevent you from enjoying this magnificent wildlife management area. Taking a few basic precautions will lessen the risk of contracting Lyme disease.

From left to right: black legged tick, dog tick, lone star tick

First, what is a tick? Ticks are tiny parasites that feed on the blood of mammals, birds and reptiles. There are over eight hundred and fifty different species in the world. They are divided between two families: hard ticks (Ixodidae), and soft ticks (Argasidae). Ticks transmit the widest variety of pathogens of any blood sucking arthropod, including bacteria, rickettsiae, protozoa, and viruses.[42]

All ticks go through three life stages. Larvae emerge from an egg with six legs. After having their first blood meal, they develop into nymphs, which have eight legs. After a second blood meal, they molt into the adult stage, still with eight legs. They will then have their third and final blood meal. At that point, the female will lay a single batch containing thousands of eggs and then die. Males will die after reproduction. The entire cycle can last from one year in warmer climates to several years in colder areas, with three years being the average.

Ticks do not jump or fly. They find their blood meals through a process known as "questing". Ticks are stimulated by heat, movement and the release of certain biochemicals, such carbon dioxide – which is exhaled by mammals.[43] The questing tick will perch on the edges of vegetation with their front legs extended. When the host brushes against these front legs, the tick will climb on and seek a suitable feeding site.

Some ticks will use one host for all three life cycles; others will seek a second or third host. Each blood meal may last from a few days to several weeks. Ticks have tiny razor-like projections with which they pierce the victim's skin to draw blood. Many hard ticks also secrete a substance that "glues" the tick in place while feeding and dissolves afterward. While feeding, the tick's outer body layer, called the cuticle, will stretch to accommodate the engorged tick. Ticks' bodies can increase up to six hundred percent of their original size during feeding.

The most common ticks in this area are black legged ticks (*Ixodes scapularis*), American dog ticks (*Dermacentor variabilis*), lone star ticks (*Amblyomma americanum*) and brown dog ticks (*Rhipicephalus sanguineus*). The black legged tick is what most of us call a "deer tick". However, field mice have been found to be the primary carriers or spreaders of black legged ticks not deer.

Black legged ticks prefer wooded habitat, sandy soils, high grassy areas and open fields. Eighty-five percent of them favor mature woods with a dense undergrowth of shrubs.[44] They have even been found in large numbers on the beaches along the southern shore of Long Island, New York – sandy areas studded by dune grass and other vegetation.

The life cycle of the black legged tick takes about two years to complete. The larvae are the size of the head of a pin and stay near ground level. Because of this, humans rarely provide their first blood meal – chipmunks, voles, mice and shrews are more commonly their victims. Animals carrying Lyme disease will infect the tick as it feeds. It will then be passed on in its subsequent meals. Peak activity time for black legged tick larvae in this area is August.

Nymphs are the size of a poppy seed. They will typically feed on birds, raccoons, squirrels, domestic animals and humans. Late May to June is the mostly likely time to be bitten by a black legged nymph in this area. Seventy percent of all Lyme disease cases occur from nymphs.[45]

The adults are the size of a sesame seed prior to engorgement. They are most active in October and November. If they do not find a blood meal before frost they will become inactive during the winter and seek a host when spring comes. Typical hosts for this stage of the life cycle are horses, cattle, deer and humans. Adult males are black in color and the females have a brick-red abdomen.

Two of the biggest threats from ticks in this area are Lyme disease and Rocky Mountain Spotted Fever. Lyme disease is transmitted by black legged ticks. An infected tick must feed for at least twenty-four hours before it can transmit Lyme disease to its victim. Therefore, the best prevention to developing Lyme disease is to perform daily tick checks.

Wearing light colored clothing in the woods helps you spot ticks easily. Tuck socks over pants legs to prevent ticks from crawling up under your pants. Using tick repellent on clothes and skin can prevent ticks from climbing aboard. Sprays containing the chemical N,N-diethylmeta-tolumide, called DEET, will repel most ticks. However, some people are allergic to DEET and others may have skin sensitivity to it. Some people develop headaches from using it.

Another solution is permethrin, which is made from the chemical pyrethrin found in some flowers. Permethrin belongs to a group of man-made pesticides called pyrethroids. This ingredient can only be used on clothing, however. Clothes should be sprayed until damp and then left to dry before wearing. The chemical will last through several launderings but should be lightly reapplied each time as an extra precaution.

Insecticides authorized for tick control include: Sevin (carbaryl), Permethrin (a pyrethroid), Dursban (chlorpyrifos), Diazinon (spectracide), Tempo II (another pyrethroid) and Damminix. These chemicals may pose some risk to humans, especially children, wildlife and domestic pets. They should be used only when necessary and applied by professionals. Keep in mind that any chemicals have the potential filter down into the water table.

There are many natural remedies that have their followers. Avon's Skin-So-Soft, for example, has so many fans that the manufacturer now totes this use in its ad campaigns. Skin-So-Soft Oil, as well as their Skin-So-Soft Lotion is rubbed onto the skin as a tick deterrent. Rubbing oil of peppermint onto the skin is another favorite method of some people.

Showers should be taken after a walk in the woods, especially during the peak summer months. Extra attention should be paid to ankles, groin, underarms and scalp area. Performing tick checks with a buddy will help insure that hard-to-see areas are checked properly. Parents should check their children and get them in the habit of daily tick checks after playing outdoors. Freezing ticks at zero degrees for at least forty-eight hours will kill them.

Ticks should be removed by tweezers. Gently twist the tick to release its grip while pulling backward and up in a steady motion. Do not apply alcohol, petroleum jelly, nail polish, hot matches, and cigarette lighters to the tick. Don't squeeze the tick, either, as these methods may cause it to regurgitate its stomach contents, include pathogens containing Lyme disease.

For identification purposes, ticks should be placed in a small, sealed container, such as an empty film canister. Add a moist, not wet, cotton ball to the container and bring it to the county cooperative extension office for identification.

If you opt not to have the tick identified, they should be wrapped in duct tape before being discarded in the trash.

Lyme disease causes a wide range of symptoms, many of which mimic other diseases, making identification difficult. One or two courses of antibiotic treatment will usually treat the disease, if caught early. Generally, antibiotics such as doxycycline or amoxicillin are prescribed for a three to four week period.

However, because antibiotics were so freely given in the past for a host of diseases, even before determining if it is was the best course of treatment, doctors are now seeing strains of bacteria that are resistant to today's antibiotics. Doctors are being more cautious of prescribing them unless they are clearly indicated, so antibiotics will not usually be ordered for suspicion of Lyme disease until positive blood test results come back.

Those with Lyme disease often test negative in the early stages because the antibodies to Lyme disease have not built up to a sufficient enough level in their bloodstream for a positive result. If symptoms persist, retesting should be done.

The most characteristic symptom of Lyme disease is a bulls-eye rash, which is usually two inches or more in diameter. Over half of Lyme disease victims will develop this rash at the site of the bite. Other symptoms can include fatigue, headaches, joint pain and swelling, muscle aches and flu-like symptoms.

If you suspect that you may have Lyme disease, see a physician immediately. Untreated symptoms may require stronger and lengthier treatments, including intravenous antibiotics and hospitalization. Even when caught in its earliest stages, recovery may take months. However, those treated early and successfully often have no reoccurrence of symptoms and can live full, productive lives.

My athletic nineteen-year-old daughter was stricken with Lyme disease. She noticed redness and swelling on her foot, but did not find any ticks and attributed it to a spider bite. When flu-like symptoms did not subside after a few days, she sought medical advice. The initial blood test came back negative for Lyme disease. When it came back positive a few weeks later, antibiotic treatment was begun. Most of the symptoms subsided shortly after that, but she was plagued by fatigue and joint pain for almost a year. It took another six months until she regained full strength back in her muscles. Today, she is asymptomatic but wary of wooded areas.

Rocky Mountain Spotted Fever typically starts with headache, fever and muscle pain. These symptoms are usually followed by a rash of black dots. It was first identified in Idaho in 1896 and was called "black measles" because of the rash's appearance.

Dr. Howard T. Ricketts was the first to isolate the cause of Rocky Mountain Spotted Fever – a bacterium later named *Rickettsia rickettsii* in his honor. The bacteria is carried and spread by hard ticks. Dr. Ricketts died of typhus – a related disease – shortly after completing his research.

The disease's name is inaccurate, as it is not confined to the Rocky Mountain region as first thought but actually exists throughout most of the United States, as well as southern Canada, Central America and parts of South America.

Treatment includes tetracycline antibiotics, however, even with treatment, fatalities occur in three to five percent of the cases. Rocky Mountain Spotted Fever is not limited to humans – my dog was diagnosed with it several years ago. Fortunately, she was able to be treated successfully with a two week course of antibiotics and suffered no ill effects.

Another disease spread by black legged ticks is human granulocytic ehrlichiosis (HGE). This disease affects humans and horses and its symptoms are similar to those of Lyme disease. Diagnosis can be made by a blood test and treated with a course of antibiotics.

Mosquitoes are not only annoying, but can also pose health risks. Most of the diseases caused by mosquitoes, such as yellow fever and malaria, do not affect people in the northeast geographic region. Many are restricted to areas in Africa and some other tropical locations.

However, in this area, arboviral encephalitides are a concern. This category encompasses all viruses transmitted by blood-feeding arthropods, which include mosquitoes and ticks. All viruses in this group are zoonotic, meaning they mainly affect and are transmitted by animals. Humans are considered "accidental victims" – they can be afflicted by the disease, but cannot transmit it to others or pass it down to offspring.

Arboviral encephalitides are distributed globally, but there are six which are commonly found in the United States: Eastern equine encephalitis (EEE), Western equine encephalitis (WEE), St. Louis encephalitis (SLE), La Crosse encephalitis (LAC), West Nile Virus (WNV), and Powassan (POW). The first four are transmitted by mosquitoes, the last two by ticks. A new virus, similar in strain to Powassan, is caused by black legged ticks.

Eastern equine encephalitis afflicts mostly horses and humans. It was first identified in 1930s and is localized to the east coast, Gulf Coast and areas in the Midwest. It is common among horses in the summer and fall, but less likely to affect humans.

Symptoms generally appear from four to ten days after a bite. They include fever, muscle pain and headaches, increasing in severity. It may lead to seizures, coma and in a third of patients, death. Those who recover may have permanent brain damage requiring institutional care.

Besides horses and humans, Eastern equine encephalitis can attack quail, pheasants, ostriches and emus and in rare cases, puppies.[46]

Western equine encephalitis is contained to the western part of the country and Canada.

La Crosse encephalitis was discovered in 1963 in La Crosse, Wisconsin. It has spread to several mid-Atlantic states (West Virginia, Virginia and North Carolina) and Midwestern states (Minnesota, Wisconsin, Iowa, Illinois, Indiana, and Ohio). LaCrosse encephalitis is believed to be more widespread than has been reported.

Its victims are typically under the age of sixteen. It starts with fever, headache, nausea, fatigue and vomiting and can lead to paralysis, coma, seizures and death. Fatalities are less than one percent of all reported cases.

St. Louis encephalitis is the most common mosquito-transmitted human pathogen in the United States. Although focused in the Midwest and southeast, it has been documented in every state except Alaska and Hawaii. Almost two hundred new cases are reported each year. St. Louis encephalitis is milder in children than adults. The elderly are most at risk for death from this disease.

West Nile Virus generally causes mild symptoms. It can and has been fatal in some cases, particularly where its victims had a more vulnerable immune system. The monitoring of dead birds is helping county health departments monitor the spread of the disease. Over one hundred and thirty species of birds are known to have been infected with West Nile Virus and migratory patterns are a concern for spreading the disease. West Nile Virus was first isolated in 1937 in the West Nile Province of Uganda. An outbreak in New York City during the summer of 1999 was first thought to be St. Louis encephalitis, but was later confirmed as West Nile Virus. The two diseases are very similar.

Powassan affects mainly the northern half of the United States and Canada. It was first identified in a five-year-old child who died in Ontario, Canada, in 1958. Those who recover may be plagued by lingering neurological problems.

These viruses strike mainly during the summer months. Symptoms include headaches, fever and fatigue. Some infections may develop into encephalitis – or swelling of the brain tissue – and may be fatal. Antibiotics only work against bacteria and cannot be used for viruses. There is no cure for arboviral encephalitides but treatment can be given to relieve symptoms and handle secondary infections, such as bacterial pneumonia.

Some vaccines are available in Europe and Japan, but there is no commercially available vaccine in the United States. The best protection is prevention. Reduce time outdoors during the peak mosquito hours around dusk and dawn. Wear protective clothing treated with insect repellent as discussed for ticks. Remove standing water in buckets, tires, playground equipment, birdbaths and anywhere else water may collect and become a breeding ground for mosquitoes. Repair or replace damaged window screens.

In areas where mosquitoes are problematic, aerial spraying may be undertaken. The Ocean County Mosquito Commission performs aerial spraying as needed throughout the county, including the area of Colliers Mills.

Peepers and Creepers

It sounded just like crickets. The steady, high-pitched chirping sounds that filled the air reminded me of a humid summer night. The winter chill was just starting to leave the air. An occasional robin hopped across the brown lawn, still frozen with icy dew.

The pitch would start out low and somewhat insignificant. Then it would increase and multiply, until it seemed as if all the woods were filled with crickets.

The chorus would start around dusk and continue for a few hours.

Some people have likened its sound to a nest of baby birds, chirping for its next meal. Regardless of what you associate with it, the sound is unmistakable and unforgettable once you have heard it.

Many a night, I would lay in bed, drowsy, as the chorus lulled me to sleep. Even with the windows closed, on an active night, the intensity of sound would slip past the panes.

But it was not crickets I was listening to, but a chorus of spring peepers (*Pseudacris crucifer*). Just as the robin is often the first bird seen in spring, the peepers are often the first frogs heard in this area as the weather warms.

Amazingly, this chorus is made by a frog no larger than your thumbnail. The spring peeper, while not usually seen, is easily recognized by the trademark "X" across its back. The body may be gray, green or brown and the x might not always be perfectly shaped, but it is clearly distinguishable.

It is named for its "peeping" sound. There are two subspecies, the Northern spring peeper, found throughout most of the eastern half of the United States, and the Southern spring peeper, whose range is confined to parts of Florida and Georgia.

The spring peeper can actually survive over the winter months with as much as sixty-five percent of its body water frozen.

It belongs to the *chorus frogs' genus* and is one of two chorus frogs found in the Colliers Mills area, the other being the New Jersey chorus frog.

The New Jersey chorus frog (*Pseudacris feriarum kalmi*) is another tiny frog whose sound gives the impression that he is larger than he really is. Slightly larger than the spring peeper, this frog is about one and a half inches in length.

He can be identified by three wide, clearly defined bands of color along his back and a singular stripe running the length of his body along its side. The base color may be dark brown to light gray, with brown to gray markings. Some frogs may be greenish in color. He will climb into weeds or vegetation looking for insects to eat.

The carpenter frog (*Rana virgatipes*) has been well named as his call sounds like a carpenter driving nails into a board. Colliers Mills is a favorite spot for this frog, as he likes still water, acidic swamps, sphagnum moss bogs and ponds.

The male is brown with four yellowish colored stripes running the length of his body. His belly is yellow with black or dark brown spots and the tail is grayish in color. His head is narrow. The female will lay between two hundred and six hundred eggs in standing water during the summer.

You have probably seen an American Toad (*Bufo americanus*), as it is extremely common. These toads come in a variety of colors, including reddish-brown, gray, olive green and brown. The skin has dark colored spots and prominent warts.

American toads are primarily nocturnal, hiding during the day. The best chance to see these toads is around dusk when they come out seeking insects. They will eat beetles, ants, flies, crickets, caterpillars, wasps, moths and spiders.

Each female toad will lay between 4,000 and 8,000 eggs that will hatch in three to twelve days. The tadpoles are omnivorous, while the adults are carnivorous.

The bug-eyed Eastern spadefoot (*Scaphiopus holbrooki*) is the only spadefoot found east of the Mississippi River. The toad spawns early in the spring, following a torrential downpour. They have even been seen migrating to vernal ponds *while* it is still pouring.

Eastern spadefoots have vertical pupils and brass colored irises, making their eyes stand out even more. These toads range from one and three-quarter inches to three and one-quarter inches in length. They may be green, gray, brown or light black in color, with a yellow hourglass pattern shape on their back.

They received their name from the spade shape of their inner hind feet. Front feet are slightly webbed. They live on sandy, loamy or gravel soils, in farmland and forest habitats.

The call of the green frog (*Rana clamitans*) sounds like a rubber band that has been stretched, and then snapped. Some liken it to the plucking of a banjo. Frogs typically call from the banks of a lake or pond. They will jump into the water when approached, giving a characteristic squeal.

Contrary to what you might have thought, green frogs are not always green. They have many color variations and patterns, but all have a large raised circle behind their eyes called a "tympanum." This is, in a sense, the frog's ear. Their skin coloring helps them stay camouflaged when out in the open sunbathing on a bank. They eat insects, spiders and young tadpoles.

Green frogs are what most people think of when you say the word "frog". This medium frog is extremely common and likes to lounge on vegetation when he's not sitting on the sidelines. Quite often they are seen riding on top of a lily pad.

Wood frogs (*Rana sylvatica*) can vary in color from olive green to black. Viewed from above, they almost have a diamond shaped appearance because of their angular head and the way their hind legs almost meet in a "v" shape.

The wood frog is a medium sized frog that can grow to almost three inches in length. Its gets its name from its brown body coloring that gives it almost a "wooded" appearance.

An identifying characteristic of the wood frog is the black mask around the eyes, earning it the nickname of "robber" or "bandit" frog. Wood frogs arrive shortly after spring peepers and together their calls sound like ducks quacking.

The Southern leopard frog (*Rana sphenocephala*) is best distinguished by the white dot in the center of its tympanum. The body may be green, brown, greenish-brown or greenish-yellow. It has numerous black spots all over the typically white belly. It is also characterized by two golden colored stripes running down the length of its body.

While it typically breeds in the spring, in warmer climates, it will breed all year round. When several of these frogs get together, their calls have been described as sounding as if they are chuckling.

The Fowler's toad (*Bufo woodhousei*) is one of the larger toads in this area, ranging from two and a half inches up to five inches in length. It may be yellow, green or brown in color, with a lighter stripe down the middle of its back.

It prefers sandy soil and marshes. The call of a Fowler's toad is one that you will not easily forget. It has been described as the bleat of a sheep that has a cold. This high-pitched nasal cry, ending on a slightly louder note is incredibly loud.

One summer, a very lonely male decided to make the rocks around our pond his home. Night after night, he would loudly call to what seemed like every female in the state of New Jersey. Even with the windows closed and the television turned up, we could not block out the sound of his pathetic call.

He either paired off or developed laryngitis, as his nightly courtship ritual ended after two months. Perhaps in someone else's backyard, a lonely male calls…

The gray treefrog (*Hyla versicolor*) ranges in size from one and a quarter inches to two and three-eighths inches long. Besides gray, it may also be green or brown in color. It may have several large dark blotches on the skin or under the eye. There is no color difference between the genders.

True to its name, it spends most of its life near trees. In the summer, it lives inside moist areas of hollow trees or on rotted logs. It hibernates in the winter underneath tree roots and leaves.

Currying the favor of a female gray treefrog requires stamina on the part of the male. They will call from May to August repeatedly during the night. The more participatory the male is, the more likely a female will choose him.

The gray treefrog has the chameleon's ability to change the color of his skin to blend it with the vegetation he is among at the time.

In New Jersey, the Pine Barrens tree frog (*Hyla andersonii*) is found only in the Pine Barrens. Other small populations exist in North Carolina, South Carolina, Georgia and parts of western Florida.

This brightly colored frog prefers the bark of pitch pines along swampy areas. They prefer shallow, acidic water and populations are affected by a drop in the water table or change in pH.

The skin is a bright emerald color with white edging and lavender to plum colored belly. The inside of the hind legs are a bright orange to yellow color. It is typically about an inch and a half in size, equivalent to the New Jersey Chorus Frog.

The Pine Barrens tree frog is a wonderful success story. It was recently downgraded from endangered to threatened on the state list. This resulted from strict regulations by the New Jersey Pinelands Commission that kept its habitat fairly stable. Nonetheless, it was still an exciting day for environmentalists who feared the loss of this unique little frog.

Salamanders are sometimes called "newts" and either title is fine. However, they are not lizards. These nocturnal amphibians have soft moist skin and long tails. The adults do not have external ear openings, scales or gills. Most are carnivorous, eating insects and fish.

There are three main types of salamanders: aquatic, which spends its entire life in the water; semi-aquatic, which live on land, but enter the water to breed, and terrestrial, which spend their entire lives on land.

Tiger salamanders (*Ambystoma tigrinum*) are large salamanders, averaging eight inches in length, with some reaching twelve inches or more. They spend most of their lives underground, sharing mammal burrows.

They have many color variations: green to gray with black spots, yellow with irregular thin black stripes, yellow with thick black stripes, dark brown with yellow-gold spots and black or gray with yellow spots. They generally breed early in the spring.

The two-lined salamander (*Eurycea bislineata*) is a smaller salamander, barely reaching three and a half inches in length. It may be yellow, green or brown, with two dark, slender stripes down either side, hence its name. Its back is dotted with tiny specks of black like someone sprinkled pepper on it.

It prefers streams and rocky areas and can survive in habitats from sea level to 6,000 thousand feet above sea level.

The four-toed salamander (*Hemidactylium scutatum*) is orange to reddish brown in color with various size dots of black scattered across his skin. Its belly is white. The hind legs have four toes instead of the usual five, giving it his name.

The four-toed salamander does not have lungs and instead breathes through its skin and through the roof of its mouth. It prefers sphagnum moss habitats where it can lay its eggs in the moss. The young live for a short time in the water, and then move onto the land.

Red-backed salamanders (*Plethodon cinereus*) resemble redworms when viewed from above. Like redworms, the red-backed salamander helps improve the soil. Their tunneling helps aerate the soil and opens up passageways for bugs that decompose the earth.

They have dark brown to black bodies with a bright red stripe running down the center of their body. A few are born without any stripe. Their bellies are black and white.

These salamanders will grow to about five inches in length. They are one of the few salamanders that do not spawn in the water. Red-backed salamanders lay their eggs in a cluster that hangs down from an old log or rock like a bunch of grapes. The females will mate every other year. She will guard her eggs for two months until they hatch by coiling herself around them like a snake.

It should come as no surprise after looking at the previous salamanders to learn that the red salamander (*Pseudotriton ruber*) is generally red in color. They may also be orange, reddish-orange or greenish and dotted with different shaped black spots. These salamanders are the ones most frequently seen when turning over old logs. They prefer moist marshlands or damp meadows.

The population of marbled salamander (*Ambystoma opacum*) is decreasing in New Jersey. This salamander's broad head looks disproportionate to its body. But like the previous salamanders, it is named for its appearance. The marbled salamander may have gray or white bands across a black or green background. Their belly is black and they average four inches in length. They lay their eggs on dry land in an area that will become wet. Once the area floods, the eggs will hatch.

Vernal pools have only recently been given more recognition in the fight to save prime ecological land. Vernal means "spring" and it is in this season that these pools come to life.

A vernal pool is an isolated body of water that dries up at some point during the year, typically in late summer. It cannot support fish life. Vernal pools can be natural – pockets of water in wetland areas. They can also be manmade – a depression in the ground caused by earth-moving machinery, for example. The key is that the pool holds water for at least two months of the year and dries out at some point during the year.

Why are vernal pools important? We know that amphibians need water to lay their eggs. At one point, it was thought that frogs, toads and salamanders would use the lakes and streams closest to their homes.

It is now known that several species will *only* lay their eggs in vernal ponds. This group is referred to as obligate vernal pool breeding amphibians. One of the reasons that obligate species choose vernal pools is to prevent predatory fish from devouring their young. In New Jersey, these species are:

- Eastern tiger salamander (*Ambystoma tigrinum*)
- Marbled salamander (*Ambystoma opacum*)
- Spotted salamander (*Ambystoma maculatum*)
- Jefferson salamander (*Ambystoma jeffersonianum*)
- Blue-spotted salamander (*Ambystoma laterale*)
- Wood frog (*Rana sylvatica*)
- Eastern spadefoot toad (*Scaphiopus holbrookii*)

There is a second group, known as facultative vernal pool breeding amphibians. They will also use vernal pools, but are not dependent upon them and will also use water that contains fish. These species are:

- Green frog (*Rana clamitans melanota*)
- Bullfrog (*Rana catesbiana*)
- Pickerel frog (*Rana palustris*)
- Southern leopard frog (*Rana utricularia*)
- Carpenter frog (*Rana virgatipes*)
- Northern spring peeper (*Psuedacris crucifer*)
- Northern cricket frog (*Acris crepitans*)
- New Jersey chorus frog (*Pseudacristriseriata kalmii*)

- Upland chorus frog (*Pseudacris triseriata ferarium*)
- Northern gray treefrog (*Hyla versicolor*)
- Southern gray treefrog (*Hyla chrysocelis*)
- Pine Barrens treefrog (*Hyla andersonii*)
- Four-toed salamander (*Hemidactyluim scutatum*)
- Long-tailed salamander (*Eurycea l. longicauda*)
- Wood turtle (*Glyptemys insculpta*)
- Spotted turtle (*Clemmys guttata*)
- Mud turtle (*Kinosternon subrubrum*)
- Eastern painted turtle (*Chrysemys p. picta*)
- Common snapping turtle (*Chelydra s. serpentine*)

In New Jersey, legislation was adopted to protect these vernal pools. Pools that do not have a permanent outlet, provide documented habitat for obligate or facultative species, hold water for at least two months, do not contain fish and dry up during the year, can all be certified as a vernal pool.

Because it is believed that there are thousands of these pools throughout the state, the Endangered and Nongame Species Program relies on trained volunteers to identify, monitor and report these vernal pools so they can be certified. This process will afford them protection under the New Jersey Freshwater Wetlands Protection Act.

The protection is crucial because not only are these species dependent upon these sources to breed, but a buffer zone around them also needs to be established so the species has access to travel to these pools. Because they have selected these pools for their offspring, biologists have also found that vegetation around them provides insects, camouflage and other requirements of these species.

In addition to breeding and life support, vernal pools provide habitat to many other species of amphibians, as well as reptiles, insects, plants and wildlife. In 2003, the number of certified vernal pools doubled to seven hundred and fifteen and the number of surveyed pools tripled to 3,799. Protection of these critical areas will have far-reaching effects for years to come, not only on the species affected, but others in the food chain as well.[47]

Snakes. The word alone sends fear down some people's spines. If you're one of the many people who suffer from *Ophidiophobia* – a fear of snakes – you're in good company. This phobia is one of the most common and over half the population suffers from it.

If you think your fear is irrational, but can't find a good reason to overcome it, take heart. Certain phobias, such as of snakes and spiders, may be "hard-wired" in us. These fears serve a purpose in areas where survival skills need to be honed daily.

A serpent is used in the Bible to represent evil. In slang, we use the word "snake" to describe someone whose intentions may not be honorable or who has an ulterior motive for his or her actions.

But despite the bad rap that snakes have been given, most snakes are not harmful. They keep the rodent population at bay and are rarely seen. While a snake's skin may be shiny – particularly if they shed recently – they are not "slimy", contrary to popular opinion.

Less than a fifth of the world's snakes are poisonous.[48] The snakes in North America and Europe are generally less venomous and dangerous than those in Third World countries, where most fatalities occur.

The snake with one of the most deadly toxins in the United States is the coral snake but it is a small, secretive snake that you would likely never encounter. Out of an average 45,000 snake bites in the United States annually, only 8,000 are from venomous snakes. Only nine to fifteen of these bites result in a fatality.[49]

If you are walking through the woods, they will not seek you out. A snake would rather avoid you and will generally only attack if it feels cornered or threatened. If you see a snake in your travels, the best advice is to leave it alone and keep walking. Do not try to pick up or touch a snake unless you are familiar with it and know what it is. Never hit a snake or attempt to kill it unless you are attacked first or are truly at risk.

Snakes generally prefer dark, moist areas. In Colliers Mills, you are most likely to find snakes in underground holes, tree cavities, moist grasslands or wooded areas with filtered sunlight. You might see them on the side of the road or on top of a log if they are trying to warm themselves.

Snakes are cold-blooded. This means that they cannot maintain a steady body temperature on their own like mammals and humans. Their temperature mimics the surroundings they are in. So snakes bask in the sun and move to warmer locations to raise their temperature and seek out cooler spots when they want to lower it.

Snakes are carnivorous. They will eat mice and rats and sometimes fish or birds. Larger snakes, such as some of the constrictors and pythons, can consume animals as large as a pig. They will not eat if their body temperature is too cool. Snakes can go for weeks without food if necessary, but most prefer a medium-size meal every few days. It doesn't matter to the snake whether the prey is alive or dead.

Snakes shed their skin every one to three months. You can tell when a snake is getting ready to shed because their eyes will appear cloudy and their skin will have a dull color. They remove their skin by rubbing against something rough, like a rock or log.

Snakes are susceptible to ticks, mites, parasites, worm, viruses and bacteria. They can even get cancer.

During the summer months, snakes are most active in the early morning or at dusk. They can be found basking out in the open in the mid to late morning. In Colliers Mills, this will typically be along a sandy road or a flat topped rock.

Later on, when the sun gets higher in the sky, look for a cooler spot to find them hiding in. Pay particular attention to logs, bark or wood, such as old railroad ties, that may be lying in vegetation.

Snakes are found in this area from April to October. During the colder weather, they will hibernate.

One final note about snakes – many people see the flicking of their tongues as a warning signal. Nothing can be further from the truth. Snakes use their tongues to collect and process data. When they stick out their tongues, chemicals in the air accumulate on them. They draw the tongues back into their mouths and into two openings of the Jacobsen's Organ. This is the reason why their tongues are forked. The organ – which is located on the roof of their mouth - processes this chemical information and relays it to the brain.

Now if learning about snakes hasn't made you uncomfortable, let's look at the snakes that you may encounter in Colliers Mills, should you be lucky enough to find one.

The Eastern garter snake (*Thamnophis sirtalis sirtalis*) is found throughout New Jersey and is most likely the snake you will find in Colliers Mills, as it is one of the more common snakes in this area. Its length is from eighteen to twenty-six inches and typically with three yellowish stripes running alongside its body.

But garter snakes come in a wide variety of patterns and colors and it may have a checkered pattern instead of stripes. The body color may be black, brown, green or olive. Its underside is green or yellow with two rows of indistinct black spots.

It prefers moist areas along meadows, marshes or streams. The garter snake is a relatively docile snake that doesn't mind being picked up unless it feels threatened. Because of its small size and popularity, it is often a meal for larger snakes. Garter snakes can give birth to as many as seventy-three young at one time.

The Eastern ribbon snake *(Thamnophis sauritis sauritis)* may be mistaken for an Eastern garter snake, as they are both the same size. The Eastern ribbon snake also prefers moist habitats. It is often found swimming along the surface of the water. Like the garter snake, the ribbon snake usually has three yellow stripes running along its dark body. Its underside is a yellow or greenish color.

Ribbon snakes, true to their name, are very slender and not as thick-bodied as the garter snake, which is the best way to tell these two snakes apart. The tail of a ribbon snake is much longer than the tails of other types of snakes; comprising almost a third of the ribbon snake's full length.

The Northern black racer (*Coluber constrictor constrictor*) is another snake that you are likely to encounter in Colliers Mills. This snake is easily identified by its black, shiny appearance and incredible speed. Rarely will you catch more than a glimpse of this snake as it quickly slithers away.

The Northern black racer can be an aggressive snake that can put up a good fight if threatened. Youngsters have a blotchy pattern that disappears as they mature. Racers can be found in woodland and grassy areas. Its length is from three to five feet. The iris is brown or dark amber.

The corn snake (*Elaphe guttata guttata)* is an example of what happens when fear gets the best of people. Once common throughout New Jersey, the corn snake is now on the state's threatened list because people frequently killed it. It is a fairly docile snake.

It prefers sandy, forested areas and pine-oak woodland. Its range is limited to the pinelands these days and its presence has been noted in Colliers Mills. It is mainly nocturnal during the summer months.

It is thirty to forty-eight inches long with red or orange patches outlined in black. The body's base color is gray, orange or brown. Its underside is black and white checkered and its tail is striped.

Some people mistakenly believe that poisonous water moccasins live in our water. Most likely, they are confusing this snake with the Northern water snake (*Nerodia sipedon sipedon*), which is common in this area. It can inflict a painful bite if disturbed, which is probably what caused the confusion between the two species.

This two to three and a half foot long snake is typically brown or black, with a slightly banding pattern. In youngsters, this banding will be bright reddish-brown, which will dull as they age.

It is an excellent swimmer both underwater and on the surface. Its main diet is salamanders, tadpoles and frogs, but some have been known to eat small mammals and birds.

The Northern redbelly snake (*Storeria occipitomaculata occipitomaculata*), true to its name, has a red belly. It may have three pale-colored but well-defined spots on its neck. The snake is usually brown with four thin darker stripes along its side. It may also be gray or black, although this is less common. In very rare cases, the underside may be bluish-black instead of red.

Northern redbelly snakes are eight to ten inches in length. They are often found in wooded areas or near sphagnum bogs, which are common in Colliers Mills.

The Northern brown or DeKay's snake (*Storeria dekayi dekayi*) likes to hide. They are sometimes mistaken for a young garter snake, as their length is only nine to thirteen inches. Usual habitat is moist woods, bogs and swamps and they have even been found hiding beneath trash that has been dumped.

Their color varies from dark brown or deep reddish-brown to a light yellowish-brown or gray. The belly can be pink, brown or yellow. It has two parallel rows of black spots running the length of its back that can help identify this species.

The black rat snake (*Elaphe obsoleta obsoleta*) has a shiny black skin like the Northern black racer, but that's where the similarity ends. Its belly may be gray and white, brown and white or yellow. The throat has a distinctive black and white checkered pattern.

Black rat snakes are good climbers and may nest in hollow trees. Its length is from forty-two to seventy-two inches.

The rough green snake (*Opheodrys aestivus*) tends to blend in with its background. They spend most of their time climbing and their light green skin often matches the vines and shrubs they slither across. It is a small, slender snake of twenty-two to thirty-two inches in length.

The Eastern hognose snake (*Heterodon platyrhinos*) loves to roll over and "play dead" if it feels threatened. This is the easiest way to identify this snake. Its upturned, hog-like nose is another clue.

Eastern hognose snakes may be jet-black to golden or gray in color. Their length is from twenty to thirty-three inches long. Its belly has a green or gray mottled pattern on a yellow, pink or gray background.

The Northern pine snake (*Pituophis melanoleucus melanoleucus*) is the only state threatened species. Its length is from forty-eight to sixty-six inches long. The body has blotches of black or dark brown on a white, gray or cream-colored background. These blotches may lighten toward the tail.

This snake's habitat is limited to the New Jersey Pine Barrens as it prefers the sandy soil. It is very secretive and likes to burrow in the sand. If threatened, it may hiss.

The timber rattlesnake (*Crotalus horridus*) is the only venomous snake found in New Jersey. It is also a state endangered species, so the likelihood of you encountering this snake is minimal at best. There are some scattered populations in the pine-oak forests and swamps of the Pine Barrens. They like to den along riverbeds.

Their length is from three to five feet long and they have two color variations. The first may be completely black or a dark brown or brownish-black.

The second type is yellow with dark brown or black crossbands. These bands may form a v-shape that changes into spots further down its back.

It is the only rattlesnake in New Jersey and in most of the Northeast. Rattlesnakes are one of the most easily identifiable snakes, even for the novice, because of its namesake rattle located on the end of its tail. It will shake this rattle as a warning.

Female rattlesnakes reach maturity at a late age and usually only reproduce once every three to four years. Additionally, less offspring are born to rattlesnakes, making the species more likely to become endangered or threatened.

Since the species has been documented in the Pine Barrens, the Pinelands Commission, along with the Endangered and Nongame Species Program began a monitoring program in 2001. The ambitious three-year program seeks to locate the dens of this species, as well as track and monitor the movements of any rattlesnakes they find.

Biologists will capture, outfit with radio transmitters and return any rattlesnakes they find during this study. Daily monitoring will be done using low-flying aircraft equipped with telemetry equipment. It is hoped that from studying and learning more about this species of snake, efforts can be undertaken to prevent its extinction.

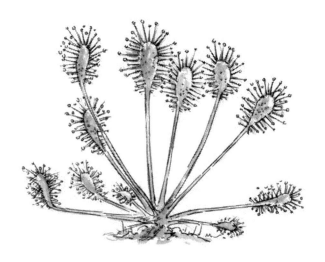

Pineland Plants

After a walk in the woods, most of us are lucky if we can recall the names of a handful of plants that we saw. Yet, if you stop in the woods and really look around, you will discover literally dozens of different species of plants in just a few square feet.

One day, I had the pleasure of walking with two well-respected botanists through a portion of Colliers Mills. I started writing down the names of the plants as they called them out, but it was a formidable task. After a few minutes, they stopped me and told me that they would forward me a list.

Most professionals will identify plants by the scientific name, which is generally two words long. The reason for this is that there are so many common names, sometimes different ones for the same plant and sometimes the same name for different plants! To avoid confusion, using the scientific name will ensure that everyone is discussing the exact same plant.

What is a scientific name? You have probably seen or heard these Latin words before. I have also placed them after the common names in this book. Botanical or scientific names are always italicized and the first letter of the first word is capitalized.

The first word in the name is the genus that the particular plant belongs to. Think of this as a person's last name. Genus is a broad category that flora with certain similar characteristics will fit into.

The second word, which is not capitalized, is the species. You can think of this as a person's first name. The species name separates plants into related but distinctly separate entities. Most people don't look closely at plants. If you look carefully, you will see that there are many notable characteristics.

Is it a tree, shrub, vine, or herbaceous plant? Trees, shrubs, and some vines are woody. Herbaceous plants are not. Vines may trail or climb.

If it has flowers, are they radially symmetrical, with many identical parts radiating from a central point, and how many parts does it have? Or are the flowers made up of different shaped parts? And what color are the flowers?

Are the leaves arranged alternately along the stem, opposite each other, or in whorls of three or more? Or are leaves absent, or only present at the base of the plant? Is the plant grasslike?

Are the leaves veins net-veined or parallel-veined? Is the entire leaf edge smooth, toothed, lobed, or dissected? Do the leaves attach to the stem on petioles (stems) or are they attached directly to the plant? What shape are the leaves?

Note the texture of the leaves, stems, and flower parts. Is any part of the plant hairy? Or scabrous (rough)? Or smooth? Or sticky? Are the stems angled or round? Is the plant past flowering and in seed? What do the seeds look like?

This might seem like a lot of work, but it is just a matter of noticing the details. As you get more familiar with how the leaves are attached, how the plant emerges from the ground and characteristics of its flowers, you will see details you never noticed before. Suddenly, it will no longer be "a red flowered plant with dark green leaves" but "a plant with dark green heart shaped leaves that alternate along its woody stem that produces a bright red flower with clusters of five petals in a star shape".

Believe it or not, if you decide to spend time studying and identifying plants, this process will become automatic, also. You will no longer think about each step – what color are the flowers, how many parts do they have, how are the leaves shaped, how are they arranged, and so forth.

Once you've learned to recognize the various plant characteristics, there are several field guides to wild plants that can help you to name your discoveries. Good ones for this area include *Newcomb's Wildflower Guide* (ISBN# 0316604429), *A Field Guide to Wildflowers-Northeastern/Northcentral North America* (ISBN# 0395183251) Howard Boyd's *Field Guide to the Pine Barrens* (ISBN# 0937548197) is another excellent choice.

Biotic communities, as defined by scientist Edward O. Wilson, are "all organisms – plants, animals, and microorganisms – that live in a particular habitat and affect one another as part of the food web or through their various influences on the physical environment."[50] Plant communities are found within biotic communities and are made up of plants only. Much diversity is found in Colliers Mills among its plant communities.

Almost nineteen percent of New Jersey is wetlands.[51] Plants that live in these communities are called hydrophytes. Different government agencies use different criteria for determining what constitutes a wetland. Generally, it is considered a transitionary area between upland and aquatic areas.

A more exact definition is offered by four government agencies, including the Environmental Protection Agency and the Department of Agriculture. The narrower definition states the wetlands have specific hydric soil types, hydrophytes (plants adapted to wetland conditions), and or water within eighteen inches of the surface for at least seven days during the growing season. Not all wetlands have peat-based soil.

Plant communities are defined by many variables. Even plants belonging to the same type of community, say for example – upland forest – may differ from one to another, depending on individual conditions that may have affected it, such as fire frequency, soil type, climate, elevation and moisture regime.

Broadly defined plant communities, such as upland forest, can be further broken down. In New Jersey, there is the northern mixed oak forest of the Highlands region, consisting mainly of white, black oak and chestnut oak, mixed with hemlock type hardwoods.

The Inner Coastal Plain is home to coastal plain mixed oak forests of white and black oak with beeches.

The Pine Barrens of the Outer Coastal Plain contains pine-oak, oak, pine, and oak-pine upland forests. The fire ecology of the Pine Barrens is the main reason for the preponderance of pine, which can make a more rapid comeback than the slower growing oaks. The pitch pine – the most fire resistant tree – can make up as much as eighty percent of these forests.

The pine-oak forest tends to be relatively open. It is often characterized by dense underbrush of early lowbush blueberry (*Vaccinium pallidum*), sheep (*Kalmia angustifolia*) and mountain laurel (*Kalmia latifolia*), black huckleberry (*Gaylussacia baccata*) and scrub oak (*Quercus ilicifolia*). Relatively few species of herbs grow here.

In a few areas of Colliers Mills, where oak-dominated forest exist, the oaks that found are here are black (*Quercus velutina*), scarlet (*Quercus coccinea*), chestnut (*Quercus prinus*), white (*Quercus alba*) and post (*Quercus stellata*). Occasionally hickories (*Carya spp.*), Sassafras (*Sassafras albidum*), Eastern red cedar (*Juniperus virginiand*) and wild black cherry (*Prunus serotina*) may also be found scattered throughout the upland forest.

Colliers Mills is also home to pitch pine lowland forest, typically bordering on the swamps, seeps, wet swales, and lakeshores. These forests generally contain pitch pine, red maple (*Acer rubrum*), sour gum (*Nyssa sylvatica*) and occasional Atlantic white cedar (*Chamaecyparis thyoides*).

Shrubs in this plant community are generally inkberry (*Ilex glabra*), high bush blueberry (*Vaccinium corymbosum*), sweet pepperbush (*Clethra alnifolia*), swamp azalea (*Rhododendron viscosum*), sheep laurel, fetterbush (*Eubotrys racemosa*), leatherleaf (*Chamaedaphne calyculata*) and sand myrtle. Wintergreen (*Gaultheria procumbens*), occasional bracken fern (*Pteridium aquilinum*), turkeybeard (*Xerophyllum asphodeloides*) and sphagnum moss (*Sphagnum spp.*) can also be found in pitch pine lowlands. Bracken fern is more often found in drier woods, like pine and oak.

Freshwater marshes can be seen along some of the lakes in Colliers Mills. Phragmites (*Phragmites australis*) and cattails dominate these marshes today. Because of the standing water found here, few trees and woody shrubs are found in these communities.

Phragmites, also called common reed, is found in every continental state in the country. It can reach up to six meters in height and is easily recognized by the tawny silken flowers along the tops of the stems. Plants can reproduce sexually via windblown pollen and produce seeds, but generally they reproduce asexually through spreading rhizomes in the soil, making for thick clusters of plants.

This grass species has become a major problem in wetlands in much of the eastern United States. The native, non-invasive strain of phragmites is believed to have existed for over 3,000 years in North America. However, in the late 19th and early 20th century, the common reed began dominating freshwater marshes. Other marsh species were choked out. Mud flats disappeared, and with them many of the wading birds that used the flats to hunt for small fish and aquatics.

Phragmites generally get a toehold where land has been disturbed — for housing developments, road work, lake dredging or other activity that disturbs the plants that are currently rooted there.

Through further investigation, it was discovered that the native species lineage was being mixed with a more aggressive strain of introduced European phragmites. Genetic studies confirmed this and in some areas, such as in New England, the genetic pools are made up completely of this non-native strain.[52]

Originally, introduced species were brought here accidentally in the ballasts of ships, or as food plants, or as impurities in crop seeds. Today, many are purchased for ornamental purposes. A recent survey of local nurseries in the northern New Jersey area revealed that eight out of the top ten best sellers were non-native species.

Occasionally, these introduced species escape and may dominate a plant community, since their natural controls, such as insect pests or plant diseases may not be found here. Native plants have evolved along with the checks and balances that keep them from overtaking a community. They may be a popular food plant for animal, bird, or insect species, and/or be susceptible to plant disease. Some native plants quickly lose footholds to these newer species, gradually changing the community's balance.

As long as people continue to purchase these introduced species for landscaping or land management purposes, the danger of invasion to our native plant communities will continue.

Some invasive plant species that were deliberately introduced include multiflora rose *(Rosa multiflora)*, Japanese barberry (*Berberis thunbergii*), Japanese honeysuckle (*Lonicera japonica*), autumn olive (*Elaeagnus umbellate*), Morrow's honeysuckle (*Lonicera morrowii*) tree of heaven (*Ailanthus altissima*), Japanese knotweed (*Polygonum cuspidatum*) and purple loosestrife *(Lythrum salicaria)*.

There are probably more species from the grass family present in Colliers Mills than from any other plant family. Several large plots at this wildlife management area are planted with grasses to provide food, cover and nesting habitat for wildlife. Many of these grasses are native; others are non-native to the area but do well in the poor Pine Barrens soil.

Other grass species volunteer – their seeds may be present as contaminants in the planted seed, or in the soil seed bank. Seeds may be blown in by the wind, carried in on car tires or transported by animals or birds.

Some of the more common grasses, found in these fields, with their scientific names are:

Wild ryes	*Lolium and Elymus spp.*
Three-awn grasses	*Aristida spp.*
Haigrasses	*Aira spp.*
Switchgrass	*anicum virgatum.*
Panic grasses	*Panicum spp. & Dichanthelium spp.*
Big bluestem	*Andropogon gerardi*
Orchard grass	*Dactylis glomeratus*
Purpletop or greasegrass	*Tridens flavus*
Bent grasses	*Agrostis spp.*
Reed canary grass	*Phalaris arundinaceum*
Brome grasses	*Bromus spp.*
Little bluestem	*Schizachyrium scoparium*
Indian grass	*Sorghastrum nutans*
Foxtails	*Setaria spp.*
Blue grasses	*Poa spp.*
Love grasses	*Eragrostis spp.*
Fescues	*Festuca spp.*
Crabgrasses	*Digitaria spp.*
Common reed	*Phragmites australis*
Broom sedge	*Andropogon virginicus*

(The abbreviation spp. denotes more than one species)

The graminoids, a collective term for the grass-like plants belonging to the grass, sedge, and rush families, are difficult for beginners to identify. But you may know more than you think about grasses. Most of us think of grass as the plants that grow in our lawns and need an annoying amount of attention in the form of fertilizing, mowing, and weeding.

What many don't realize is that corn, rice, barley, oats, wheat, millet, and sorghum are grasses, which feed the majority of the world's population. Some species are annual, meaning they will die at the end of the season, and others, perennial, which will return on their own, year after year. In cooler climates with frost conditions during winter – the zone that Colliers Mills is in – perennial grasses will turn brown and die back during the winter. New growth will come up from the roots when spring arrives.

Some grasses respond to extreme heat and lack of moisture by shutting down chlorophyll production, as you may have seen in your lawn during summer droughts and heat waves. Prolonged heat without rain may kill the plants' roots.

You may pick up little ditties or other memory tricks to help you learn the differences between grass-like plants. If you learned to play guitar, you probably recall "Every Good Boy Does Fine" to help you with the string names. Here's one you'll quickly learn:

"Sedges have edges,
grasses have joints,
rushes are round
from the top to the ground."

You may find this particular ditty helpful in learning your way around seemingly similar green plants. "Sedges have edges" because in some, their stems are actually triangular shaped instead of round like grass and rushes. However, this ditty is somewhat broad-based and there are exceptions to every rule.

Not every sedge has an "edge;"; some are actually rounded, like grass or rushes. Sedges differ from grass and rushes in that their leaves are 'three ranked"; they generally have three rows of leaves extending out in different directions. Looking down on a sedge plant from above, you'll see leaves extending out from the stem at one hundred and twenty degree angles from each other, like the spokes on a wheel.

Sedge flowers are very tiny and do not have petals. If you wish to learn to distinguish between them, you will need to carry a magnifying glass for identification.

Sedges and grasses serve an important role in places like the Pine Barrens where fires, either prescribed (set and controlled) or wild, are not uncommon. A low intensity fire makes them sprout vigorously and grow densely. This rapid growth is important to prevent soil erosion from the bare, burnt ground.

Sedges and grasses also provide nutrition for wildlife, such as waterfowl, deer and small mammals. This is crucial for their survival immediately following a fire, as most of their other food sources have been destroyed and will take time to replenish.

Some sedges are tolerant of shade but most prefer moist conditions. They are often found in Colliers Mills in the low-lying wetlands areas where the ground is damp and they receive filtered light through the tree canopy.

One widespread common sedge tends to grow in dry woods. Pennsylvania sedge (*Carex pensylvanica*) can be found throughout much of the upland wooded areas at Colliers Mills. But many need or thrive only in full sun.

Native Americans used sedges to make baskets and mats. Their extremely strong fibers have also been used to make rope, when superior strength was needed.

Rushes are perennial plants that are usually found alongside bodies of water or in shallow water. Their dense cluster of roots helps to stabilize the shoreline and prevent erosion. They prefer soils of sand, clay or gravel.

Rushes grow from one to eight feet high and generally have slender, stiff round stems. They provide a hiding place and food for birds, waterfowl and fish, which like to eat rush seeds. Small mammals, such as rabbits and mice also enjoy the seeds. Muskrats will eat both the seeds and roots of these plants. Amphibians and fish will often spawn among rushes.

You will see several varieties of clover in Colliers Mills, typically growing alongside the grasses in the open fields. The sweet smell of clover attracts bees, which help pollinate other plants. *Lespedeza cuneata*, or Chinese bush clover, is abundant in some of the planted fields at Colliers Mills. An introduced species, Chinese bush clover was brought to the United States from Asia. It was cultivated in the southeastern states, but has escaped, and is now established in disturbed sites and along roadsides. This is an example of how introduced species can unexpectedly become a threat to native vegetation.

Clover has valuable assets as well. Clover species have nitrogen-fixing bacteria that live in nodules in their roots. These bacteria reduce nitrogen from the air and in the soil into a form that they and other plants can use to synthesize plant protein, nucleic acids, and chlorophyll.

Colliers Mills is home to several hundred plant species. Wetlands areas offer reeds, rushes, sedges, cattails and sundews; mesic woods abound with sheep laurel, blueberries, huckleberries, ferns, and spotted wintergreen, and upland woods are home to oaks and pitch pines, mountain laurel, huckleberries and bayberry.

A field trip for the Torrey Botanical Society was led by field botanist Linda Kelly through Colliers Mills on July 28, 2001. The purpose of the trip was to identify the species seen by the group that day. Dr. William Standaert served as an unofficial recording secretary, and created the partial list of the plants encountered that day, which is included in Appendix C. This list contains only a sampling of plants encountered during the trip and is not indicative of the variety and number of species present throughout Colliers Mills.

Milkweed is perhaps best known to butterfly lovers as food for the monarch butterfly. This is the only plant that monarchs will lay their eggs on and the maturing larvae will digest. As they eat the leaves, they ingest chemicals that will make them distasteful to predators. These chemicals do not harm the larvae, but can prove toxic to humans and livestock. Milkweed gets its name from its thick, white sap that leaks out when a stem is broken and resembles milk.

Monarchs are poisonous to predators and it is believed that their bright colors serve as a warning to those considering them for a meal. If the toxins are ingested, they can cause weakness, vomiting, fever, difficulty breathing, muscle spasms and coma.

Butterflies that are similar in color and pattern – the queen and the viceroy – are not poisonous, but rely on the similar coloration to confuse predators into avoiding them. This adaptation is called protective mimicry.

Colliers Mills is home to a few species of milkweed, including swamp milkweed (*Asclepias incarnata*), common milkweed (*Asclepias syriaca*) and butterfly milkweed (*Asclepias tuberosa*) also known as butterfly weed. Swamp milkweed is a wetland plant found along the edges of damp swales, wet meadows and along lake edges. In the summer and fall, it produces clusters of pinkish colored flowers.

Its seeds have long hairs called comas, which catch the wind and help disperse the seed. They are also soft and were used for stuffing pillows and lifejackets, during the World War II. The leaves may cause dermatitis to humans.

The stems of the common milkweed contain fibers strong enough to be used as rope. It is propagated from seed as well as underground shoots and can be invasive. It prefers sandy, clay or rocky soils. It can be found on the edges of forest, open fields and dry roadsides. It prefers full sun. The flowers are purplish-white and bloom from May to August.

Native Americans used the common milkweed as medicine. The Cherokee drank a tea made from the roots to cure backaches. The sap was used for bee stings, warts and ringworm by the Cherokee, Iroquois and Rappahannock. The Cherokee also used it as a laxative, an antidote for mastitis and to treat venereal disease.

The Chippewa mixed the root with food to produce postpartum milk flow. The Iroquois made compounds from the leaves to prevent hemorrhaging after childbirth and to treat stomach ailments. The Menominee ingested the flower buds for chest discomfort. The Meskwaki used it as a contraceptive and the Mohawk used it to produce a concoction that induced temporary sterility. [53]

Butterfly milkweed (or butterfly weed) is a much lower growing perennial than the two species previously mentioned and is typically found along dry roadsides and fields. It can tolerate damp, but not wet, soil conditions. Its bright orange to reddish-orange flowers almost rival the colors of the monarch. It differs from the other two milkweeds in that it has alternate rather than opposite leaves. It grows slowly and blooms in mid-summer.

We don't usually think of plants as being carnivorous, but that's what sundews are. Like the Venus flytrap satire in *Little Shop of Horrors*, sundews trap insects and then devour them. Actually, what really happens is that their plant juices break down the insects' bodies and then absorb the nutrients from them.

These "man-eating" plants are typically found in acidic, nutrient-poor wetlands. In Colliers Mills, sundews can be along the lake edges, in sphagnum moss, on bare sandy or muddy ground, and growing out hummocks or rotting logs.

A sundew's leaves are edged with red tentacles that are coated with a sticky secretion that traps insects. Shining like dew drops in the sun, insects make the deadly mistake of thinking these secretions are nectar.

Colliers Mills is home to three species: the spatulate-leaved sundew (*Drosera intermedia*) which appears to have tiny spatulas for leaves, the thread-leaved sundew (*Drosera filiformis*) which has elongate, erect, slender leaves, and the round-leaved sundew (*Drosera rotundifolia*), which as the name implies, has leaves shaped like rounded spoons. Sundews populations are found scattered throughout North American, Europe and Asia.

The spatulate-leaved sundew grows two to eight inches in height and produces white flowers throughout the summer. This sundew is able to tolerate wetter conditions than the other two species.

The thread-leaved sundew is the largest of the American sundews. Its leaves may grow up to seven inches long. Its pink flowers, beckoning to pollinators, develop above and away from the leaves, as it would not be advantageous to trap and digest the insects that pollinate the plant's flowers. Dragonflies and damselflies will perch on the flowers to look for insects.

The round-leaved sundew holds its leaves out in a rosette pattern, like hands outstretched for a present. It averages two to four inches in height, with white or pink flowers opening one at a time. Of the three types of sundews found at Colliers Mills, it is the least tolerant of inundation and usually found on slightly higher ground.

Another interesting carnivore found in Colliers Mills is the bladderwort (*Utricularia*) These unusual plants make up the largest genus of carnivorous plants and are the most widespread. Approximately two hundred and fourteen species are believed to exist worldwide.

These aquatic plants lack true roots. In most bladderwort species, the majority of the plant is submerged in water, where it floats freely.The name bladderwort gets its name from the empty pouchlike sacs or bladders that transverse the lower stem. These bladders have tiny hairs, which catch and trap small water prey, such as mosquito larvae, water ticks and aquatic worms. The hairs also serve to prevent water debris from washing into the bladder.

Bladderworts typically produce small yellow or purple flowers on stems above the water. Most bladderworts are yellow. The two species with purple flowers are rare.

The entrance to the bladder is sealed watertight by glands in the bladder that continuously pump water out to maintain the pressure on the seal. The entrance is surrounded by another set of tinier, stiff hairs. When prey is attracted and trapped by the larger, upper hairs and brush against the entrance hairs, the entrance door will openly inwardly, sucking the prey in with the force of the water. The entrance closes within 1/30th of a second, trapping the prey inside.

The meal is digested by plant enzymes over a period of several days; however, the trap is ready to catch another meal within thirty minutes of its last capture.

Common yarrow (*Achillea millefolium*) is an introduced species from Eurasia, although a few other yarrow species are native to the United States. It is the only yarrow seen throughout the fields and meadows in Colliers Mills. It spreads quickly through its root system and can be quite invasive.

As plants go, it isn't very demanding. It's not fussy about the soil it grows in as long as it has good drainage. It prefers full sun, but will grow in partial shade. It is resistant to drought, insects and disease. It will grow to three feet tall, with long, green feathery leaves that look like parsley on the edges. The flowers are white, flat-topped clusters that bloom from early summer until fall and are slightly fragrant.

Used externally, yarrow is styptic, which means it stops bleeding. The genus name, Achillea, honors Achilles, who according to Greek legend, used the plant to staunch the bleeding of his warriors in battle. [54]

It has also been used as an herb to lessen menstruation, an astringent, an antiseptic and an anti-inflammatory. As a tonic, it has been used as an antibiotic, an analgesic, to lower blood pressure and to stimulate digestion. The reason for its varied uses is the more than one hundred active biological compounds it contains, including menthol, insulin, quercetin, salicylic acid and camphor.

Besides its medicinal purposes, yarrow is also used in food. The leaves and flowers can be used for seasoning. Immature leaves are put into salad and the plant has also been used to flavor beer, wine and soda.

Animals usually avoid yarrow and will only eat the flowers. If cows ingest it, their milk will have a bitter taste. Some people are allergic to yarrow and ingesting too much of it can cause photosensitivity.

The black-eyed Susan (*Rudbeckia hirta*) is an easy plant for the novice to recognize. With its bright yellow daisy-like petals and fuzzy dark brown centers, this cheery flower is well-known for its famous childhood ditty – "...*she loves me, she loves me not...*". Readily available in nurseries and garden centers, it is a common landscaping plant.

This member of the aster family can be either perennial or biennial, depending on the environment. Biennials grow for two years but only flower in their second year.

Each flower head contains from ten to twenty ray flowers (petals) and the plant will continue to produce flowers profusely all summer until frost. In the wild, flower heads can be up to three inches across.

Black-eyed Susans are found in open fields, woods, along roadsides and in disturbed areas. They grow all across the continental United States, except for the Southwest. This native species attracts many types of butterflies.

The genus was named after Olaus Rudbeck, a Swedish physician and botanist. He preceded Carolus Linnaeus, the inventor of the system of scientific names that is in use today.

Goldenrods (*Solidago* spp) are well known, yellow-flowered plants. However, they have been considered the bane of allergy sufferers – a reputation they don't deserve. For years, people who suffered from "hay fever" – late summer allergies – have blamed goldenrod for their condition. Just as these plants burst into bloom, the symptoms of sufferers peak. But it isn't goldenrod that is causing the problem, but a nondescript looking plant called ragweed, which blooms at the same time.

Goldenrod is a member of the Aster family. It is a hardy plant typically found in fields and along roadsides. It generally prefers full sun that does not require a lot of water and will grow in average soil; however some species are shade tolerant. Goldenrod is highly adaptable and there are even species that can grow in wetlands and tolerate "wet feet."

There are at least eight different species found in Colliers Mills. Found throughout North America, goldenrod will reach heights of one to seven feet. Its long plumes of showy bright golden flowers produce pollen too heavy to become airborne, according to botanists. The bright yellow flowers were used to make dye at one time. Goldenrods are resistant to most diseases and pests.

In another touch of nature's irony, the genus name for rag-weed (*Ambrosia artemisiifolia*) means "food of the gods". Yet, it is this plant that causes so many allergy and asthma sufferers misery. Ragweed grows throughout the northern and eastern parts of the United States. It reaches a height of one to seven feet tall and grows profusely. Its tooth-like segmented leaves resemble those of the marigold when it first breaks through the soil, but quickly distinguishes itself. The ragged shape of these leaves is what gives the plant its common name. Stems and leaves may be smooth or hairy.

The fruit of this plant is a main staple of the bobwhite quail's diet. The tiny flowers bloom in late summer and release yellow pollen that is light enough to be carried by air. Most of the plants responsible for allergies have airborne pollen. Those plants with sticky, heavier pollen rely on insects to physically transport the pollen from plant to plant. Male flowers are generally yellow and located at the top of the plant, female flowers are below them on the same plant and usually white in color.

While many of the plants in Colliers Mills are beautiful to behold and worth locating, there are some that you are better off not encountering. These include poison ivy (*Toxicodendron radicans*) and poison sumac (*Toxicodendron vernix*). The oils of these plants, called urushiol, can be irritating to the skin's surface, causing a nasty rash and severe itching. Urushiol is very potent; the amount contained in a space the size of the head of a pin is enough to produce itching in five hundred people.[55]

The oil is water insoluble, meaning that you can't wash them off with water alone. Soap, which attaches to the oil molecules and allows them to be washed away with water, must be used. Care should be taken not to spread the oils to other areas as you are washing them off. You should use cold water if available, as hot water opens the pores and can let the oil seep into the skin.

The urushiol oils will penetrate the outer skin surface or epidermis, within three to thirty minutes on the average. So if they are not washed off before this time elapses, the oils will continue to cause a reaction no matter how thoroughly you wash the area with soap. Blisters erupt later on that can last for a few weeks. For this reason, a small bottle of liquid soap should be carried with you in the woods so you can begin cleaning the area immediately.

The oils can also be transferred onto clothing and be contacted by skin later on, as they last a long time. Oils can even remain active for up to five years on a dead plant.

Some people are more allergic to these oils than others and the slightest contact can produce a severe reaction. It is the most common allergy in the United States, with a substantial percentage of the population being allergic to some degree. Usually, reactions increase with exposure and your first brush with poison ivy may not even produce a rash. Sensitivity can also change over time and with exposure. As you age, you may lose your sensitivity to these poisons.

Urushiol is contained inside of the plant's capillaries, which must be broken to release the oil. However, this does not mean that if you handle the plant carefully, you will not fall victim. Remember, a minute dose can cause a reaction and you cannot tell if a capillary has been broken somewhere on the plant and transported by insects to the surface of the leaf you are touching. The oils can also become airborne, especially if the capillaries are damaged by fire then blown into the air or a lawnmower cuts and scatters them.

Urushiol can be found in the plant's leaves, stems or roots. It is a clear to yellow color when inside the plant or when it first is exposed to the air. Later, it becomes a brownish-black color. Patches of oil that remain on the plant's leaves may look like furniture varnish. The name comes from the Japanese word, *urushi,* meaning lacquer.

There are many folk remedies to treat a reaction from one of these plants, including the use of rubbing alcohol, vitamin E, antiperspirant and more. Some say that heat is effective for healing skin blisters and recommend spending time in the sun or taking very hot showers.

Others recommend exposing the rash to the air and still others suggest keeping it covered with bandages. One common thread among most of these treatments is to make the blisters dry out as quickly as possible, which of course, will stop the itching.

Topical antihistamines and cortisone applications – both external and internal — purport to ease the itching. Generally, what works for one individual may not for another, so you'll probably have to use the trial and error method. Scratching may also cause an infection. If you feel you have a bad case, see a doctor immediately. Steroids may be prescribed to suppress the histamines that your body is producing.

Since the first edition of this book came out, I have contracted poison ivy twice. After employing the various methods and suggestions I first wrote about, I discovered a "new" treatment that has proven most effective to me and many other sufferers.

Holding the affected area under water as hot as you can tolerate (please be careful about not burning your skin) will open up the pores and allow the histamines to come to the skin's surface and be flushed away. When the water first hits your skin you will feel intense itching but this will soon subside. Repeat this procedure on all of the affected areas at the same time until the itching has completely subsided.

From what I read in several forums on the Internet, it will take your body roughly six to eight hours to produce more histamine in your body. Since histamine is what causes the itch, you will have relief for all of the hours until it is replenished, allowing you to work, get a good night's sleep, etc. I can't vouch for the facts or results using this method, but I can testify that it has brought myself and others great relief.

Still, the best medicine for poisonous plants is avoidance. Learn what these plants look like in various seasons so you can steer clear of them when hiking. Fortunately, each is pretty distinctive once you have seen them. Try looking them up in a guide with photo identifications and review them before each walk to commit them to memory.

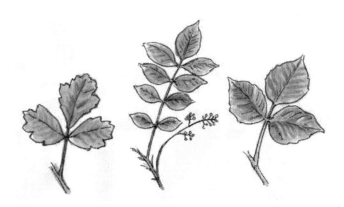

(left to right) Poison oak, Poison summac, Poison ivy

Poison ivy is the most common in this area. You may have heard the saying, *"Leaves of three, let them be,"* used to warn of this plant. Poison ivy actually has groups of three leaflets, of asymmetrical shape, on each leaf. The edge of each leaflet may be different as well – with one smooth and the others with tiny serrated edges. The middle leaflet is on a longer stalk than the other two and all three are pointed at the ends.

The leaves are a reddish color in the spring, green in the summer and may turn yellow, orange or red in the fall. It also produces small, white berries. These are found in the fall, growing in small clusters very close to the main stems.

It generally grows as a shrub or a vine in this region and can get rather thick. It doesn't attach with tendrils like the grape and briars do, nor does it twist around other plants like honeysuckle is inclined to do. Rather, the vine is covered by numerous hairs, called aerial rootlets, which adhere to whatever supporting structure (including trees) the vine grows on. The rootlets are thinner and more scattered on younger plants and thick on older growth. Poison ivy is generally most recognizable as it emerges because the oil gives its leaves a shiny appearance.

Eastern poison oak (*Toxicodendron toxicarium*) looks very similar to poison ivy. Its leaves may have a more lobbed appearance, like an oak tree. It generally grows in the western part of the United States, although there is an Eastern version that is believed to grow in this area, although not found in Colliers Mills. It may grow as a vine or shrub with the same three characteristic leaflets. Eastern poison oak prefers sandy soil and areas ravaged by fire, explaining its presence in the Pine Barrens. Its leaves and stems may have a fuzzy appearance, owing to fine hairs growing on the surface.

Poison sumac is a small tree, which can grow to a height of over twenty feet tall with a distinctive reddish stem. It prefers sphagnum bogs and swampy areas in which to grow. It has from seven to thirteen symmetrical leaflets on each leaf. The leaflets are much more slender than those of the poison ivy or oak.

The whitish berries of the poison sumac grow in long drooping clusters that dangle down past the leaves on long stems. Other sumacs, which are non-poisonous, have large, erect, dense clusters of fruit growing from their branch tips, have a green stem and their leaves are arranged in an alternating pattern.

Towering Timber

Trees are a vital natural resource that most of us take for granted. The value of trees to our well-being is immeasurable. Trees, like all plants, absorb carbon dioxide along with pollutants and release oxygen back into air. People, on the other hand, retain oxygen that gets distributed throughout the body and expel carbon dioxide through our lungs. Amazingly, a single shade tree can produce enough oxygen for ten people!

Trees also provide shade and serve as windbreaks. Their roots help prevent soil erosion and stabilize the banks of streams and rivers. Forests act as sponges, soaking up rain and snow to recharge the aquifers below.

Ever step into a forest on a hot day and immediately notice a drop in temperature? That is due to the process of evapotranspiration performed by the trees. You may have also noticed the quiet. Trees absorb sound. A stand of trees can reduce highway noise by as much as ten decibels.

A walk in the woods can be invigorating, whether it's early spring when the buds are beginning to break or an eerily quiet tromp through freshly fallen snow. Many people plan their hikes in the fall when the vibrant colors flood their visual senses.

Most people believe that the leaves of hardwood trees change color due to the arrival of frost. Native American Indian lore told of a more "colorful" tale – that celestial hunters had killed the Great Bear. The red leaves were tinged by his dripping blood; yellow and orange came from the grease splashing onto the leaves as the hunters cooked their feast.

But the real reason why leaves change color is due to chlorophyll production decreasing. Chlorophyll is the green pigment that allows leaves to absorb energy from sunlight and use it to break down carbon dioxide and water into carbohydrates. This allows for the trees' growth in spring and summer.

In addition to chlorophyll, carotenoid pigments are also found in the leaves. This is what gives carrots their orange color. As chlorophyll production slows and eventually halts, the green pigment disappears, making the carotenoid pigment – which was present all along – visible to the eye.

The leaves also contain other pigments, such as anthocyanin, which produces a color range from red to blue. Different tree species have varying amounts of these pigments, giving rise to brown oak leaves, red-colored dogwoods and orange splashed sugar maples.

As the leaves fall to the ground and decompose, they release nutrients into the soil, such as calcium and potassium. The tree will use these again in the spring for growth so the advent of autumn is really just one phase in the well-planned cycle of nature.

Almost half of New Jersey is covered by forest, even though it is the most densely populated state in the country. Despite exploding population trends, its 2.1 million acres of forest has remained fairly constant. The reason for this is that urban areas still attract the greatest number of inhabitants.

Even with a loss of over a million acres of farmland since 1956, most farmlands that have been lost to development still maintain an open portion of land. Towns have become more restrictive and may require buffers while some municipalities ask for a portion of land to be preserved as dedicated open space.

Eighty-eight percent or almost 1.9 million acres of New Jersey's forest is classified as timberland. At one time, most of the trees in Colliers Mills were removed for this purpose. Due to more stringent regulation and inclusion of many of these areas such as Colliers Mills into protection programs, the amount of timberland available throughout the Garden State has remained relatively constant over the past three decades.

Ocean County maintains over sixty percent of forest. This is mainly due to the Pine Barrens presence in this county.

In 1999, a state survey identified seventy-seven different species of trees in New Jersey. Pitch pine was the most common, closely followed by the Northern red oak – our state tree – and other members of the oak family, including white, black, pin, blackjack, scarlet and chestnut oak. Red maple constituted thirteen percent of the inventory.

This composition of trees is closely mirrored in Colliers Mills, with pitch pine and various oaks leading the pack. Underbrush consists mainly of scrub oak, huckleberry and blueberry in the southern end and clusters of mountain laurel in the northern end of Colliers Mills. Scattered stands of Atlantic white cedar line the swamps that are present throughout Colliers Mills.

Since pine trees are the most common trees in the Pine Barrens, how does a novice tell them apart? One way to start is by looking at the leaves, called needles. They may be straight or twisted. Do they come in clusters of two, or three? Notice also where the needles appear – are they only at the end of the branches, along the branches or come out from the trunk? What color are the needles and how long?

You can also look at the bark of the tree. Note its color, texture and if it has scales or the type of bark that peels off. Pine cones can often help identify the type of pine tree that they fell from – note the size and shape. Oaks can be distinguished by their leaves and acorns – again, the size and shape - as well as the cap style on the acorn.

Leaves, of course, are probably one of the easier ways to help identify species. Field guides are extremely helpful in this respect. First, you need to familiarize yourself with the terminology so you can describe the leaf properly and understand the description.

If each leaf consists of several leaflets arranged along a central stem, it is compound leaf. If the leaves appear directly opposite each other on the twig, these are "opposite leaves". If they are staggered instead, they are "alternate leaves".

By studying the guides and with practice, you will become more adept at telling the different species apart. Don't be discouraged if the trees you are looking at don't exactly match the examples in your field guides. All sorts of conditions can alter a tree's appearance from a textbook example – age, pollution, insect damage, and overcrowding to name a few. What you're looking for is basic identifying characteristics, not perfect matches. With experience, it will get easier.

The range of the pitch pine (*Pinus rigida)* -- mascot of the Pine Barrens -- stretches southward all the way to North Carolina. It is highly tolerant of poor, sandy soils. In New Jersey, its range is limited to acidic, often sandy, infertile soils that are periodically burned by fire.

It is easily identified by its dark, thick scaled bark and scraggy offshoots of branches. Its shape is often irregular and contorted.

The needles are stout, rigid and gathered in bundles of three. They are dark-green and slightly twisted, two to five inches in length, with a point on the end.

We already looked at the pitch pine and its adaptation to fire. But this is not the only unique adaptation that this tree has. Red squirrels feast heavily on the cone's seeds. In areas of high red squirrel populations, the pitch pine will produce less seeds.

The seeds are also preferred by birds such as quail, chickadees and juncos as well as mice, but these do not pose the same level of threat that the squirrels do. Their populations have no effect on the quantity of seed production.

Shortleaf pine (*Pinus echinata)* can be mistaken for pitch pine because its bark has the same thick dark scales. However, the scales of the shortleaf pine are longer and more rectangular. Its wood is used for rough construction lumber, crates, pulpwood and low-grade furniture.

Its needles are straight, slender, flexible and dark green to blue-green in color. They are three to four inches in length and grouped in mostly clusters of two or sometimes three.

The shortleaf pine is the second most common pine tree in the pinelands. In New Jersey, it is found in sandy, acidic uplands and is tolerant of infrequent fire. Its shape is more filled out and less gangly than the pitch pine and the two species are frequently found together.

Virginia pine (*Pinus virginiana)* is also known as Jersey yellow pine, scrub pine, North Carolina pine and spruce pine. Its branches are less scrawny in appearance than pitch pine and its short, stiff, stout needles are in pairs. They are dark green or grayish-green and often twisted. Their one to three inch needles are the shortest of any pine tree grown in New Jersey. Their cones are typically small and favored by several songbirds and mammals.

Virginia pines tend to have a majestic, old world look about them. They typically reach heights of fifty to seventy-five feet, although they can grow as tall as one hundred and twenty-two feet. Its irregular branching pattern often contains dead branches. Its flat, scaly bark tends to be lighter in color than the pitch pine, often with an orange hue.

Their shallow roots tolerate a variety of soil conditions, from sandstone to acidic, marine deposits to limestone. But they are not tolerant of shade. Virginia pines are one of the first trees to take over an open field and are often planted in areas where strip mining has occurred. However, as taller trees mature around them, they will die out from lack of sun.

Their range extends from northeastern Mississippi to parts of Long Island, New York. The Virginia pine sawfly is its biggest enemy and its larvae can defoliate an entire mature tree within two years. Immature larvae feed on the outside of the needles, leaving a straw-like center. Mature larvae will consume the entire needle, as well as the bark and the bud.

Red maple trees (*Acer rubrum*) appear frequently throughout Colliers Mills. When you were in the primary grades in school and made rubbings of leaves, most likely maples were used. A maple's leaves can resemble a hand, with the rounded palm representing the base of the leaf, and the fingers each lobe protruding out on the leaf.

The trees are also used for shade, ornamental value and lumber. Squirrels and many varieties of birds enjoy their fruit, called samaras. Its twigs are enjoyed by rabbits and white-tail deer.

Red maples have smooth gray bark when young and broken darker bark when older. Their leaves have between three and five lobes. They will reach heights between twenty and forty feet.

Colliers Mills also has a few silver maples (*Acer saccharinum*). The leaves are distinguished from the red maple by a deeper notch in between the lobes. They are also whitened in appearance and may be hairier underneath. Silver maples produce greenish flowers, whereas the red maple has red flowers. The silver maple is a much taller tree, reaching heights of forty to sixty feet, with the tallest having reached one hundred and twenty feet. Its bark is gray and may flake, leaving brown spots underneath.

(left to right) Leaves from a maple tree, red oak and white oak

In late September, as cooler breezes chill the air, the acorns begin falling from the oaks. Providing a high-energy treat for the coming winter, squirrels begin gathering them in abandonment and burying them. Colliers Mills is home to several types of oaks: red, southern red, white, chestnut, post, scarlet, willow, black, pin, blackjack, scrub and dwarf chestnut.

Oaks are among the tallest trees in the forest and often the oldest. The largest white oak in the United States was the Wye Oak, believed to be more than four hundred and sixty years old. It was declared Maryland's State Tree in 1941 and it was the first time in American history that a government agency purchased and preserved a single tree. Before it toppled during a thunderstorm in 2002, the tree measured three hundred and eighty-two feet in circumference and ninety-six feet tall. In case you're trying to picture what a tree that size would look like, its crown measured almost a third of an acre!

In 1940, the American Forestry Association held a nationwide contest to locate the largest living specimens of this country's trees. The Wye Oak was the first tree to be nominated.

New Jersey is home to several famous old oaks as well, most notably the Salem Oak of Salem County. It is a sixty-one foot white oak whose circumference measures two hundred and fifty-eight inches at the standard measured height of four and a half feet tall. It is four hundred and nineteen years old and it is believed that John Fenwick treatied with Native Americans under its branches in 1675.[56]

There are two main groups of oaks — "red" and "white". The different varieties of oak can be distinguished by their leaves and acorns. Those in the "red" oak group — Northern red, pin, black, scarlet and southern red — have bristle-tipped leaves and acorns that take two years to mature. "White" oaks have rounded leaf lobes and acorns that mature in one season. They include white, swamp white, chestnut, scrub, blackjack and post oak. The acorns of a red oak are bitter and usually inedible; those of the white are sweet and eagerly savored.

Oaks are slow growing trees that provide almost half of all the hardwood production in this country. Their steady, slow growth produces almost uniform rings that are popular in furniture and flooring. The trees are also fairly disease and insect resistant.

While pines and oaks are often seen together, the question of which will ultimately dominate is predicated on several variables — fire frequently being the primary one. Oak trees will begin to dominate pine forests where fires are infrequent because the rapidly growing oaks will quickly shade out the pine trees. It is also harder for pinecone seeds to germinate in the leaf litter left by the oaks. However, natural or prescribed burning will kill off the oaks and allow the pines trees the opportunity to repopulate the area once more.

The Northern red oak (*Quercus rubra*) was adopted as New Jersey's state tree on June 13, 1950. Governor Alfred E. Driscoll stated in part, in his proclamation, "the red oak is a representative tree of New Jersey with beauty of structure, strength, dignity and long life, that it is most useful commercially and enjoys great freedom from disease, that it is adapted to our New Jersey soils and is compatible with all native shrubs and evergreens, permitting lawn and grass areas to be successfully grown under its canopy, and that the fall color of its foliage places it foremost in our natural landscape scene."[57]

It is a medium to large sized tree with a rounded crown. It will often crowd out other trees and prefers lower, northern facing slopes with well-drained, fertile soil. This soil is found throughout Colliers Mills, although concentrated more in the northern end.

This tree's range is throughout the eastern half of the United States, with the exception of the Deep South. It is capable of surviving three hundred to five hundred years, although it would be unusual to find a tree of that age. Northern red oak is not fire tolerant and is somewhat sensitive to drought, but trees killed off in either of these manners will often resprout from the roots, which remain safe below the ground.

Native Americans used its acorns as a source of protein, fat and starch. They would crush the acorns and wash them in hot water to remove the tannins and other acidic compounds before eating them.

The wood is highly prized for furniture, railroad ties, housing beams, flooring and bridge timber.

After losing a giant chestnut oak to the developer's bulldozer, the Mercer County Soil Conservation District did some research. They were able to convince the Department of Environmental Protection to fund the protection of unusually large trees under the Clean Water Act. [58]

Since the trees help reduce rainfall runoff and recharge groundwater, they were in essence, protecting water quality. So the District was awarded a grant for further study. They used Global Positioning Data (GPD/GIS) to map all the large trees in their watershed district, which included part of Mercer, Monmouth and Hunterdon counties.

They created a database that catalogued each large tree in the district, along with a photograph and a block and lot number corresponding to the municipal tax map. By creating this database, developers with computer access can learn in advance if the property they are looking to build on has any trees, which may be affected. By protecting the trees, water quality is also maintained, soil erosion is reduced and building costs for the developer are minimized.

The Mercer County Soil Conservation District is hoping that their program will spread to the rest of the state. Currently, the only protection afforded to large trees is that enacted on the municipal level through local ordinances.

The Eastern red cedar (*Juniperus virginiana*) and the Atlantic white cedar are not related. The Eastern red cedar is actually a member of the pine family and is easily identified from the Atlantic white cedar by its reddish-brown bark and twigs. The Eastern red cedar generally prefers upland, but can survive in wetlands and poor, dry soil. It is mainly found on the eastern half of the United States and is the only evergreen found in Kansas.

The female trees produce berries that are bluish-gray and waxy. Birds often depend on these for a winter food source although the berries have a pungent odor when crushed. Birds will usually swallow the berries whole and the one to four seeds are deposited nearby after passing through the bird's gut intact. The majority of Eastern red cedar is propagated this way.

The male trees produce very tiny cones that will release pollen just before spring starts. If you swat the branches at this time, a smoky cloud of pollen will escape.

Today, its wood is used for furniture such as chests, wood carvings, pencils, railroad ties and fence posts. The scent of its wood is very fragrant but unpleasant to moths and it is often used as a natural insect repellent. The wood is also rot resistant, making ideal for outdoor furniture. Cardinals will often tear strips of its bark to use for nesting material.

The Atlantic white cedar (*Chamaecyparis thyoides*) is mostly found in swamps along the Coastal Plain and is sometimes referred to as Jersey cedar or swamp cedar. It is a member of the cypress family. The primary uses for its wood are canoes, boat building, fence posts, log cabins, shingles and utility poles; the latter because of its straight, tall trunk. Its bark may be reddish-brown like the Eastern red cedar, but it most commonly a whitish-gray color.

It typically reaches a height of eighty to eighty-five feet with a two foot diameter, but has grown as tall as one hundred and twenty feet with a five foot diameter.[59]

Atlantic white cedar trees are typically clustered together in stands, often so close that it is hard to distinguish where one tree ends and another begins. It is believed that over 100,000 acres of white cedar swamps were present in the 1930's; today there are only approximately 38,400 acres left in New Jersey.

Like the pine trees, Atlantic white cedar seeds rely on fire ecology for survival. Fire will kill the Atlantic white cedar trees themselves, but their seeds will rapidly germinate after a moderate, severe or short-lived fire. Controlled burning practices to reduce widespread forest fires are believed to have contributed to the declining population of these trees.

In New Jersey, Atlantic white cedar stands are often found on the site of former cranberry bogs. They are a vital resource to the Pine Barrens for several reasons:

- Filtering and purification of water
- Prime habitat for threatened and endangered species such as swamp pink, timber rattlesnakes who den in their roots, and the Pine Barrens tree frog
- They can support almost twice the number of nesting birds than any other tree species.

Birch trees are pioneer trees, particularly in the pinelands. They were one of the first trees to appear after the land was clear-cut. On the edges of woods, one can see birch grow in Colliers Mills.

One of the main jobs of pioneer trees is to improve the soil. This is accomplished by their deep roots, which draw nutrients from the soil into the leaves and bark. When the leaves fall and decompose, their nutrients are returned to the soil, only now in the upper layers where other trees with shallow roots can obtain them. It is estimated that a mature grove of birches can produce between three and four tons of leaf litter per year.

Like most pioneer trees, birches prefer full sun. They do not tolerate overcrowding and will die out as the area populates with other species. They also enjoy sandy soil, which allows their roots to go deep. The root system of a healthy birch can occupy a distance twice the tree's height. Another way of looking at this is a mature birch's roots can cover a third of a football field.[60]

To satisfy this extensive root system, birches need a lot of moisture. In one day, the roots of a mature birch can draw enough water from the soil to fill ten bathtubs! This is why you will find most birch alongside streams, rivers, lakes and ponds. There is a beautiful gray birch near the side of Success Lake where the waterfowlers association meets to practice.

Soil fungi have a symbiotic or mutually beneficial relationship with birch —as well as oak and pine — attaching themselves to the roots and bark where they break down organic matter in the soil into nutrients like nitrogen and phosphorus which help the tree grow.

Some fungi can actually filter toxins and prevent them from reaching the plant. Others protect plants from drought, insects and bacteria. Fungi also store large amounts of carbon and may provide the key to slowing down global warming.

Birches provide food for at least three hundred and thirty-four different animal species, from caterpillars to deer. Birds like the pine siskin enjoy its seeds, while white-tailed deer enjoy nibbling on the twigs.

Leaf buds and twigs appear in April and are reddish-purple in color. The leaves are bright green at first, then dull. In the fall, they may be yellow or brown, depending on the birch species. The leaves are somewhat triangular in shape, with sawtooth edges.

Birches are monoecious, meaning that each tree contains both male and female flowers. Male flowers are trailing two-inch long catkins, while the female flowers are small and upright. Wind helps to pollinate the trees. Each catkin has tiny seeds with wing-like projections that catch and are carried by the breeze. A mature birch can produce up to a million seeds in a year, but only a small amount of these actually develop into trees. Most sprout near the parent tree, but sometimes the wind can carry the seeds for a great distance.

The name "birch" means "bark". The trees were used to build canoes. Gray birch is a narrower species reaching thirty-five to fifty feet in height. The trunk may split into several smaller trunks. It prefers the edges of lakes, woods and fields. In New Jersey, this species is found only in the northern counties.

White birches were used to make paper. It generally reaches forty to fifty feet in height, although it can grow as tall as eighty feet. Its bark sometimes looks as though it is peeling and dark patches are often seen under the white skin. These darker areas are the lenticels or breathing pores of the bark. As the tree grows, these stretch out and may look like claw marks.

An old Native American tale has it that a boy wandered away from the tribe and was taken to a bird's nest where he lived among the offspring. The baby birds attacked him so he killed them and ran back to his tribe. As he was running, the angry parent birds tried to catch him, so he sought refuge in the hollow of a birch tree. The marks were left by the birds' attempt to get at the boy.

An interesting hardwood tree found in Colliers Mills is the black walnut (*Juglans nigra*). It is often found around old village sites. It can reach one hundred and twenty feet tall. It has a dark furrowed bark with flattened ridges. Black walnut trees prefer a much more alkaline soil than other trees.

Its root bark gives off a toxic substance called juglone. The toxic zone radius can be as much as eighty feet from the trunk of a mature tree. Certain trees and shrubs will not grow in close proximity to a black walnut because of this substance. Shrubs such as mountain laurel, blueberry and rhododendron are particularly sensitive to this toxin and may die within two months of planting within this tree's root zone.

Pollen from these trees, which is typically released in May, can cause allergic symptoms in humans and horses. The juglone toxin is also found in the trees' leaves, bark and wood, but in much less concentration than in the roots.

Leaves from the tree can be composted because the toxin will break down in about two to four weeks when exposed to water, air and bacteria. But in soil, it can take up to two months for the juglone to degrade. Testing for remaining toxins is often done by planting tomato seeds in the soil, as the seedlings are especially sensitive to toxins.

Catkins – long trailing green flowers – hang from the branches of male trees and the branch tips in female trees. The walnuts, which measure two and a half inches in diameter, fall in autumn. Once the outside of the shell is cracked, the inside must be allowed to dry out for a few days or it will stain your hands.

The nuts can be eaten raw or cooked. When using them in recipes, the strong, smoky flavor can overpower the other ingredients, so use them sparingly.

The black willow tree (*Salix nigra*) is one of the smaller deciduous trees, reaching only forty to fifty feet in height. This rapidly growing tree will reach maturity within thirty years. It is considered a "pioneer" tree as it is one of the first to take over an abandoned field, just like Virginia pine.

It is also referred to as a swamp willow, as its shallow roots are well-suited for wet locations and along the water's edge. It is found throughout the country along stream corridors and its lateral roots help prevent soil erosion and nutrients from washing away.

The black willow is easily recognized in winter by its thin, fragile bare twigs, either golden or reddish-brown in color. Its wood is soft and light and preferred by white-tailed deer, rodents, beavers and rabbits.

The nectar from its one to three inch yellow flowers is favored by bees and butterflies. Its leaves are eaten by the caterpillars of many butterflies and moths. In turn, these insects help pollinate the tree.

It is the only large, native willow with varied human uses such as artificial limbs and a high grade of charcoal for the manufacture of gunpowder. One can imagine that these trees were quite abundant when Colliers Mills was thriving.

Magnificent Mammals

A twig snaps. You hear the brush of leaves. Then the familiar thump-thump sound of clove hooves hitting the white sugar sand.

Startling a white-tailed deer (*Odocoileus virginiamis*) is nothing new for New Jerseyans. In the fall, lovesick deer dash in front of our cars during mating season (called "rutting"). In the winter on icy roads, we swerve to avoid the startled doe that has been foraging for brush in the frozen ground. Still, there is something beautiful in that brown-eyed look of a doe standing watch over the fawn next to her. Perhaps it's a throwback to the days of childhood as we sat watching Walt Disney's *Bambi*.

It may be this memory that drives such a wedge between conservationists and hunters. Every time hunting regulations are changed, a new means of capture is developed or another area is opened for hunting, the controversy rages.

Hunters track and shoot deer for sport, food, challenge and pleasure. It is a state sanctioned sport that allows the Department of Fish and Wildlife to maintain areas such as Colliers Mills. Without the support of hunting license fees, we would not have these wildlife management areas.

Still it is a double-edged sword. The area available for deer browsing is quickly becoming scarce as housing developments gobble up woods they once claimed for their own. Newcomers to the state quickly lose their love for Bambi as prized flowerbeds are eaten and new cars are purchased to replace the ones totaled in deer collisions.

Hunters will tell you that the sport thins the herd to reduce the numbers of deer in our developments and on our roads. But is hunting the answer? What about birth control for deer? Should the population of deer be managed, or left to nature's own devices? These questions are not easily answered. It is hard to have a balance of nature when man is constantly tipping the scales.

The white-tailed deer is an efficiently built mammal. Its slender legs and agile frame allow it to move quickly and quietly through thickly wooded areas. It is quite a capable jumper, able to leap over ten foot fences without a running start.

Its range is southern Canada and all parts of the United States except the southwest, Alaska and Hawaii. It prefers wooded areas where it can browse and hide, but deer are highly adaptable and have even been seen browsing on the lawns of housing developments.

Deer can sense movement and have a good sense of smell. Hunters know to always stay downwind from deer to minimize detection. Often one deer serves as a "lookout" for the rest of the herd as it browses. If it senses danger, it will stomp its hooves in warning and flair its nostrils, making a snorting sound. It may move its ears as it quickly flicks its tail back and forth. It may also raise its tail, showing the white underside. This visible marker helps fawns follow their mothers across a field.

The other deer will look for the intruder and together they will make a decision to flee or stay. They will run in short bursts, leaping over branches and brush. Once they are a short distance away, they will stop and turn around to see if the danger is still following them. Deer can travel at speeds up to thirty miles per hour and they are also strong swimmers.

Deer know to conserve energy, particularly in the winter months. They know how far to travel to outpace most threats and will not venture further unless they feel it is necessary. Often, if the browsing spot was particularly interesting, they will return after allowing a safe time period to pass.

Deer are cautious and particular eaters. I once found my tomatoes sampled, one bite per tomato, with the familiar clove prints surrounding my plants. Did they think that the next tomato they tried would have a different taste?

Deer are herbivores or plant eaters. They have a four chambered stomach that allows them to eat plants other animals can't tolerate. Corn and apples are favorites of deer in the summer and a reason why so many farmers keep rifles on their land. In the fall, they stock up on acorns and nuts; in the winter, whatever twigs or brush is accessible without traveling too far.

Deer are creatures of habit and will often use the same trails over and over again. They have scent glands on the bottom of their feet and inside of their hind legs, which are used for mating and identification.

In New Jersey, the mating season begins in November and the does give birth in June to one to three fawns. The fawns are reddish-brown with white spots and can walk immediately after birth. They begin eating brush a few days later and are weaned from the mother at about six weeks of age.

Female fawns stay with their mothers for two years; males venture out on their own after a year. Deer will typically bed down in open grassy areas during the day, but a doe will hide her young fawns among the brush. They will lay down with their heads and necks stretched out to minimize detection from predators.

The deer's main predators today are humans. Sometimes dogs or coyotes can pose a problem. Years ago, herds were kept in check by wolves and mountain lions. Today, disease or over-browsed land is the biggest threat to herds, after humans.

Many people are concerned about deer coming in close contact with people due to deer ticks and Lyme disease. But these ticks live in brush, landing on whatever comes across their path. Studies show that deer are the victims of these ticks the same way that people are. The real threat, scientists believe, are field mice that come in contact with ticks more readily and can easily transport them from one area to another.

Red fox (*Vulpes vulpes*) are omnivores that eat fruit, berries and insects as well as small animals. Adapting to suburban life, I have seen red fox raid garbage bags and many of my neighbors have erected cages to keep their garbage in and the fox out.

Red fox on Island Beach State Park — a more natural beach on the shore with a slightly wooded entrance, became accustomed to tourists. They began walking up to cars waiting on line to enter the park, to beg for food. Eventually, since hunting was not permitted there and no natural controls were present to contain the herd, they died a horrible death from rabies and parvovirus.

Red fox are nocturnal, but will sometimes hunt during the day. Most of the time, they will use the sunlit hours to curl up and sleep with their tail covering their face. Its scent glands are located above the base of the tail.

They have exceptional hearing and can pick up the sound of an animal burrowing underground or digging in the earth. They will stalk their prey like a cat, sneaking up and then pouncing on it. Top running speed is around forty-eight miles per hour.

Fox are also lazy, preferring to sleep out in the open or use another animal's den. Their reddish brown coat, like the deer, helps it blend in among the woods.

The gestation period for the red fox is two months and the mother will give birth to one to ten kits. The male will bring food to the mother and kits until they are ready to leave the den, at about a month old. First they will eat regurgitated food, and then the mother will bring them live food to develop their hunting skills. Kits strike out on their own around seven months.

Red fox are found throughout America and Europe and scattered populations live in North Africa. They were introduced to Australia in the 19th century. Their preferred home is one of varied habitat and they are as comfortable in tundra as they are in forest and farmland. Red fox are typically solitary animals and live in the same established range for generations.

Probably the most curious thing about red fox is their method of catching rodents. They will stand perfectly still as a mouse moves about, then will leap into the air and pin the mouse down with their forefoot upon landing.

Red fox seldom attack poultry as commonly believed and their biggest threat to humans is rabies. People are really the foxes' only predator, although occasionally a wolf or coyote will kill them.

The American black bear (*Ursum americanum*) is becoming a more familiar sight around Colliers Mills as the bears extend their range southward. It was thought that the bears would not cross Interstate 195, but that apparently has not stopped them.

The black bear is a medium sized bear, weighing between one hundred and thirty-five to three hundred and fifty pounds. Their sharp claws allow them to climb trees very well. Bears have a more developed sense of smell than other animals and very good hearing, which makes up for its average eyesight.

Bears are protected in national parks and this has allowed them to become less fearful of people. More and bears are venturing into backyards to raid garbage pails. In northern New Jersey several years ago, a man offered food to a bear in order to take his picture and was scratched by the bear. Most likely, he was trying to knock the food from the man's hand, but this familiarity between bears and people can be a dangerous thing.

Bears that get used to raiding garbage cans, whether in parks or suburbia, may decide these free meals are easier than hunting. The food, of course, is not the healthiest thing for the bear's diet, and in some cases, the diet of the person who discarded it, either.

People may think of their cuddly teddy bear from childhood and forget that bears are wild animals. They are capable of attacking and mauling a person although they would rather retreat than fight. A three hundred pound angry black bear is no match for an unarmed person.

Bear's body language is conveyed by the position and action of the head. A bear walking with its head down signals aggression. An agitated bear will make a snarling noise or chomp its jaws.

Vegetation makes up the majority of a black bear's diet, although they will also eat insects and berries in the summer and acorns in the winter. They need to get an adequate supply of food before retreating into their dens for five to seven months of the year. During hibernation, the bear's temperature will drop; the heart rate will decrease to half its normal rate and other body functions will slow, as well.

Cubs are born during the winter months and will feed on protein-rich mother's milk until the spring when they leave their dens. They are born blind and deaf. Mothers will train their cubs how to hunt with various vocal sounds. The cubs will continue to learn and grow until they are about two years old, then they will go off on their own.

Groundhogs or woodchucks remind me of oversized prairie dogs. A woodchuck waits by the base of my neighbor's apple tree in the fall and clutches his prize in his two front feet as he sits up on his hindquarters. With one paw, he deftly eats the apple while looking around. He is able to do this because woodchucks have thumb stumps besides their claws, making them able to manipulate objects better than their less dexterous cousins.

Woodchucks are one of the few animals that have benefited from our encroachment upon their habitat. From open lawns to the offerings of flowers and vegetable gardens, woodchucks are as happy living alongside of us as they are in the woods.

Don't be fooled by this animal that weighs only five to fifteen pounds. Woodchucks are terrific swimmers, climbers and runners. Their tunneling ability is unmatched and they can burrow up to five feet below ground and build tunnels extending thirty feet or more! Their tunnels can crisscross and connect like an elaborate maze.

Woodchucks will double their weight in the fall, before hibernating for an average of five months. Like bears, their bodily functions will slow down during this time period.

However, woodchucks will not mate until they leave the den. Four to six babies will be born a month later. By late summer, they will be ready to live on their own.

Woodchucks like to eat grass, berries, fruit and vegetables. Fruit such as apples and pawpaws are a particular favorite.

In Colliers Mills, woodchucks are often found in the open fields or in the woods just off the dirt roads. A mound of dirt next to a deep, wide tunnel opening is a sure sign that a woodchuck has found its home.

Woodchucks are capable of several vocal sounds, including a shrill whistle to warn of nearby predators. This latter sound has earned them the nickname "whistle-pigs".

Eastern gray squirrels (*Sciurus carolinensis*) have been described as many things, one of the more common being "rats with bushy tails". These rodents, while seemingly cute when sitting back on their haunches nibbling on an acorn, cause thousands of dollars a year in home destruction.

Squirrels are also the bane of some bird watchers, who go to great lengths to discourage squirrels from helping themselves to the seed in their bird feeders.

Their antics in trying to outwit these "squirrel baffles" are sure to bring a smile to anyone's face.

If nothing else positive can be said about squirrels, one has to admit that they are incredibly agile and acrobatic. Squirrels can actually pivot their hind legs one hundred and eighty degrees so that they can turn around in a narrow space.

Squirrels have razor sharp claws that allow them to climb trees very quickly and grab onto branches as they run without losing their balance.

They are very smart and it is said that the early settlers learned which plants were safe to eat and which were toxic by watching the squirrels, who seemed to know not only which were acceptable to eat, but when they were at their peak flavor.

Squirrels have an extensive vocabulary, from barking to clicking sounds. Their tails can also be quite expressive, showing everything from curiosity to anger. Their primary use however, is for balance, especially when climbing from tree to tree or across utility lines.

There is no difference in size or coloration between the genders. They live an average of seven years, although they will live longer in captivity.

Squirrels have both a winter and summer coat and will molt twice a year. The tail only molts once a year, however, typically in July. The squirrel will grow heavier fur during the winter, particularly on his ears and the bottom of his feet.

Squirrels have four sets of whiskers: on their nose, throat, above and below the eyes. Whiskers are actually touch receptors, the way that our fingertips are, and squirrels use them to collect data about its surroundings, the way that a cat does. This may be one of the secrets to their agility and great balance.

They also have excellent eyesight, even in dim light and very good peripheral vision. Their senses of smell and hearing are also acute. Squirrels have a full set of teeth, including upper and lower incisors that grow throughout their lifetime, as with other members of the rodent family.

Like other rodents, squirrels are quite prolific. Females can have litters when they are only a few months old. Both the male and female stay reproductively active throughout their lifetimes. Squirrels are not monogamous, and females may mate with several males during the course of a day.

Squirrels are generalists, feeding on whatever is handy. Almost one hundred plants and fourteen animals are on their menu. Nuts, acorns and pinecones are particular favorites. They will even eat fungi, animal bones and frogs. We have all seen squirrels burying nuts, but often wonder if they remember where they put them. It was once believed that with enough squirrels burying nuts, they were bound to dig up someone's stash. However, some studies show that squirrels can find their own buried treasure, using their powerful sense of smell and perhaps some memory skills.

They build three different types of homes, when they're not breaking and entering into the houses of humans. One is a summer home, made of loosely woven branches in the treetops. A winter home is constructed more thoroughly, with a waterproof outer layer and a soft inner one. For the inside, fur, feathers or moss may be used. These homes are called dreys and they are built in close proximity to each other. It is believed that this clustering helps protect them from predators.

A third home is a den inside of a tree trunk, what most of us think of as "squirrel homes". Many people are surprised to learn of dreys - we don't think of squirrels building nests.

Many of us have seen squirrels darting back and forth while crossing the road and this often leads to their deaths as motorists don't know which way they are going to run. This annoying "road trick" was developed to outwit predators who are confused by their antics and not sure which direction to attack from. Unfortunately, evolution doesn't seem to have taught squirrels that cars cannot be evaded in the same manner as other predators.

"Field mice" are generalists — a name assigned to animals that eat a variety of plants as opposed to specialists who limit themselves to one particular food source. They are one of the smallest members of the rodent family.

Like other rodents, field mice can reproduce at alarming rates. A female mouse is generally pregnant every month and only has a two-week gestation period. They give birth to three to five young, who are born hairless, blind and deaf. Within a few days they can hear and within a week, their eyes open. At three weeks of age, they are ready to leave the nest.

A cousin to the rat, field mice share a number of similar characteristics. However, they do not have the long front teeth of a rat. Both are typically brownish-black or grayish-white in color. Since they are primarily nocturnal, meaning they hunt at night, their dark color helps camouflage them from predators.

They also rely on their extraordinary sense of smell, speed and size to survive. Field mice are scavengers and will eat anything they think is edible.

They also have a long list of predators willing to eat them if given the chance. The list includes owls, dogs, cats, bears, wolves, rabbits, hawks, snakes and more. To avoid predation is one of the reasons they are nocturnal.

Their tail is hairless and almost the length of their body. They use their sharp claws to dig for food and enter homes. They are able to squash their small bodies into tight spaces to avoid detection. In the open field, they will often run under bushes to avoid being sighted by an owl. Most field mice don't survive past two years.

Field mice will make nests from whatever is available – grass, twigs, soft weeds, paper and the like. They prefer to hide, so the best place to find them is under old boards, wood, trash or something of that nature.

The greatest threat from field mice, apart from the destruction they cause to homes, is the spread of disease. Notably, they serve as transport vehicles for black legged ticks, which can carry Lyme disease. Many other diseases are harbored by field mice.

Elmer Fudd, the great hunter depicted in the Warner Brothers cartoons, may have not been so far off base when he referred to this creature as a "wrascally wrabbit" as you will come to see.

The Eastern cottontail (*Sylvilagus floridanus*) is a rabbit you will typically encounter in Colliers Mills. This species ranges from southern Canada, throughout the eastern portion of the United States and into the northern part of South America. It has been introduced into parts of the western United States. It has the widest range of all rabbits.

There are several subspecies of Eastern cottontails, including the New England cottontail (*Sylvilagus transitionalis*), marsh rabbit (*Sylvilagus palustris*) and swamp rabbit (*Sylvilagus aquaticus*). The New England cottontail differs from the Eastern cottontail in that it has a black patch between its ears. A curious note about the swamp rabbit – it actually walks instead of hopping and prefers to swim.

Sometimes, rabbits are mistakenly referred to as "hares." Hares are a completely different species, with long ears and large hind legs. Jackrabbits are hares.

The Eastern cottontail lives in varied habitat, including grassland, forest, swamps, deserts and open fields. One of their defensive mechanisms is to sit perfectly still, hoping that a predator will pass them by. This actually allows you to get pretty close to rabbits in the wild, so you can see their features in detail.

Rabbits are typically seen in the early morning and again at dusk, when they forage for food. While harmless in the wild, they can be quite destructive to gardeners as they indiscriminately chew up flowerbeds and vegetables. Sprinkling of blood meal or human hair will often discourage them.

Another folk remedy is to pour used cat litter around the flowerbeds, but care must be taken not to spread bacteria to plants, where it may harm them. Also, pregnant woman should not handle used cat litter, as it can cause toxemia. If fencing is employed, it should be at least two feet high as rabbits are excellent jumpers.

The typical diet of rabbits not dining in flowerbeds is grass and clover during the warmer weather. In the winter, rabbits feed upon the bark of maples, birch, oak and dogwood trees.

The Eastern cottontail has speckled brownish-gray fur, which allows it to blend into its surroundings quite nicely. The fur is reddish-brown around their necks and shoulders and lighter on their nose and bellies. Their tails have puffy white fur on the underside, giving rise to their common name. In the winter, their fur may take on more of a grayish hue as their warmer coat fills in.

Eastern cottontails perform an elaborate and interesting mating ritual. First the male and female will chase each other. When the female is ready to mate, she will stop running and turn to face the male. Sitting back on her haunches, she will "box" at the male by waving her front paws at him. To finalize their union, one of them will jump straight up into the air, followed by the other. At this point, they will finally mate.

Most mothers "hide" their nests in plain view and they are easily found by humans, as well as predators. Many well-meaning people call animal control because they think the babies have been abandoned. The reality is that mothers only nurse their offspring for ten minutes a day, five in the early morning and five minutes at night as dusk falls. Their milk fills the babies up and they do not need additional feeding during the day.

Female rabbits build their nests out of grasses and weeds. They often line them with fur from their chest. This keeps the young warm and protected when the mothers are away from the nest. They stay away so as not to attract predators to the nest. They will usually give birth to one to nine bunnies.

Eastern cottontails are born without fur but develop a full coat within a week. They are also born blind and their eyes open around ten days of age. At three to four weeks of age, they leave the nest to explore and return at night to sleep. By seven weeks, they are on their own.

Most of us have heard the saying, "multiply like rabbits" and this is rooted in truth. Eastern cottontails can mate at three months of age and will mate again within hours of giving birth. Typically, three to four litters are produced each year.

Cats are a big threat to the young bunnies, especially domestic cats. Feral cats will kill for food; domestic cats will capture prey for play. Many a bunny has been skinned alive by a house cat looking for something to play with.

Eastern cottontails are solitary animals and very territorial. They are generally nocturnal, but may hunt during the day. They are very agile creatures, able to leap distances of ten to fifteen feet. They can obtain speeds of up to fifteen miles per hour.

While their hind legs are not as large as the jackrabbit's, they are still strong enough to support their weight and allow them to balance. Since they live among the high grass, they will often stand up on their hind feet to survey for potential predators.

Besides cats and dogs, their other predators include hawks, foxes, coyotes, eagles and weasels. You may have seen a rabbit fleeing by hopping from side to side. They do this to break their scent patterns and leave a trail that's harder to follow.

Why Conservation is Important

It goes without saying that what we don't protect today may not be here tomorrow. In large tracts of open land, such as Colliers Mills, it is easy to be lulled into thinking that water and woodland are resources too abundant to become threatened.

We need to understand and protect them while there is still time, so that future generations will have adequate supplies of clean drinking water, that threatened species will not become extinct, and that the balance of nature is maintained.

We have seen the rise and fall of charcoal, sawmill and bog iron villages in Colliers Mills. We watched the luxury of Emson's hotel and racetrack vanish into the sandy soil, and pitch pines rise from where a grand ballroom once stood.

It is perhaps that "reversal of fortune" if you will, that may persuade people not to worry about the housing developments that are sprouting up like weeds. But the villages of Emson's era are not the major infrastructures lining the roads of today.

We have in many ways become an easy-to-use, disposable society. Fast food, disposable diapers, freezer-to-microwave meals all contribute to our landfills. There is a debate over how long a disposable diaper takes to break down in landfills – some sources point to five hundred years or more[61]; others doubt the ability of them to break down at all, especially in an airtight landfill.[62]

Controversy rages over what is more economically friendly. The cotton diaper camp points to the 3.4 million tons of disposable diaper waste accumulated in 1989.[63] There is concern that viruses, bacteria and waste products from diapers in landfills will seep in the water table.

On the flip side, disposable diaper manufacturers argue about pesticides used in cotton fields and chlorine bleach used in the washing process and the ill effects that these chemicals can have upon the environment when reusable diapers are chosen instead. The battle heats up and no one is saying for sure which is the better alternative for our ecosystem.

Diapers are just a symbol of the confusion over what is more ecology-friendly. We are beginning to question the use of fossil fuels and aerosol spray cans and their possible link to holes in the ozone layer and global warming.

Even if conclusions can be drawn, it may be too late in some cases to stop or reverse the damage that has already been done. The United States Geological Survey has begun examining disturbing levels of radon, mercury and other contaminants in the wells that draw water from the aquifers below Colliers Mills.

Even with the restrictive regulations regarding building in the Pinelands National Reserve, housing surrounding the pinelands can also pose a risk. Builders often clear-cut land to allow machinery easy access, removing trees that prevent erosion.

We now know that compaction of soil from these earth-moving machines can prevent water from seeping back into the water table below. Instead, it often runs off into street sewers where it is carried out to rivers and oceans without being treated. Lawn fertilizers and chemicals, motor oil and antifreeze and other typical household containments are often found in this runoff.

It's not just up to the builders and legislators to figure this out. Each of us can do our part. Attend a public meeting of your town's environmental commission if you have one. Find out what is going on in your backyard.

Remember to recycle. In 2003, over a trillion aluminum cans

were thrown out instead of recycled at a loss of twenty-one billion dollars. Recycling is at our nation's lowest average in twenty-five years.

Today, numerous products can be recycled: cans, bottles, plastic, paper, tires and more. Shoe manufacturer Nike has embarked on an innovative program called "Reuse-A-Shoe". Used or defective shoes are collected and recycled into material for sports surfaces, such as running tracks, basketball courts and playgrounds.[64]

Lions Club International has been collecting used eyeglasses for over seventy years for redistribution to developing nations. More than 6.5 million eyeglasses were collected during their 2002-03 fiscal year.[65]

Many public and private corporations have embarked on their own unique recycling programs, accepting a wide range of products from batteries and computers to automobiles. Toxic products are accepted by county recycling centers on scheduled days throughout the year to prevent these items from being discarded in landfills.

Many products can be given away to those in need. Most hospitals and nursing homes welcome donations of used magazines. Clothing and furniture can be given to organizations such as the Salvation Army or Goodwill who will redistribute them at a reduced cost to those in need. Even food – fresh or cooked – can be collected and dispersed through soup kitchens and other programs such as Second Harvest. The latter distributes nearly two billion pounds of food each year to American communities in need.[66]

You might want to also consider composting. All food scraps except meat and dairy products – which attract rodents – can be put in the compost bin. You don't even have to buy anything fancy – just pile discarded compost into a corner of your yard.

Layering "brown" (fallen leaves, twigs, etc.) and "green" (freshly cut grass, just pulled weeds, etc.) matter will aid in composting, but it is not necessary. The key to a successful compost pile is getting the temperature hot enough at the core to "cook" the compost. This is accomplished by keeping the pile moist, locating it in an area where it will have sunlight and turning it over as often as possible to aerate it.

If your pile is very large, you might consider purchasing an aerator – an inexpensive prong that you insert into the pile and pull straight up, allowing metal tines to open up and drag air through the pile as you remove it. Another way to make sure that there are pockets of air in your pile is to intersperse small twigs and branches into the pile.

If you properly "cook" your compost, you need not worry about weeds you may have collected because the heat will destroy the seeds. To be on the safe side though, don't throw infected plant matter into the pile to avoid spreading disease.

Once your pile is done, the compost should be a soft, crumbly dark brown colored soil. This "brown gold" as it is called will contain vital minerals and nutrients that you can use to layer over your flowerbeds, mix into the soil for healthy vegetables or use in place of potting soil. You will be amazed at the quality of plants that grow from this soil and you will not need to use expensive, synthetic chemicals and fertilizers on your plants.

Volunteering is another way to help. In addition to your town's environmental committees and planning boards, many organizations welcome an extra pair of hands. Don't forget area historical societies which are typically always in need of new members and volunteers to help catalog artifacts and run events. Look on the Internet and check with your public library for the names and contact information of organizations that meet your interests.

Your county cooperative extension is another resource. In Ocean County, NJ, the cooperative extension offers Master Gardener programs as well as Master Composters. In return for the training received, each volunteer contributes a number of hours back to the community educating them on the topics they just learned about.

The New Jersey Department of Environmental Protection is always looking for volunteers. From helping with paperwork, banding waterfowl, identifying vernal ponds and more, there is a wide range of work available.

New Jersey's Department of Environmental Protection's Wildlife Conservation Corp (WCC) boosts 1,600 members whose volunteer services add up to over a million dollars a year in cost savings. Volunteers assist at hunting checkpoints, trout stocking programs, help upkeep shooting ranges in wildlife management areas and offer fishing instruction. Volunteers also work with the Endangered and Nongame Species Program offering slide presentations and participating in their Speaker's Bureau.

Anyone over eighteen years of age is welcome to join. A minimum of forty hours per year of volunteer time is requested. Volunteers work independently or alongside biologists, wildlife control representatives and researchers. They are responsible for providing their own transportation to and from the site and completing monthly reports of their hours and activities.

In recent years, the state began implementing tougher environmental laws. Endangered and threatened species were afforded certain protections, but their habitats previously had not been. Legislation was proposed and enacted to change that.

Tighter stormwater regulations were adopted in 2004 to protect the quality of drinking water. By designating certain crucial waterways as "Category One," three hundred foot buffers are now required to prevent contamination from housing developments. The measure is also designed to allow recharging of the aquifers instead of allowing runoff to occur. These enactments protect over 6,000 miles of vital waterways in the state.

Standing near the banks of the Anderson Brook, former Governor James McGreevey stated, "These stormwater rules are the most comprehensive set of water protections in the nation—no other state has required statewide three hundred foot buffers around its high quality waters. They will prove to be a critical tool in our fight against sprawl."[67]

"This is the most important and significant action taken yet to protect New Jersey's water since the passage of the Freshwater Wetlands Act in 1988," said Jeff Tittel, Executive Director of the New Jersey Chapter of the Sierra Club. "This is a huge victory for our environment."[68]

The regulations require municipalities, large complexes such as hospitals and our state's highway systems to create stormwater management plans that will protect the integrity of our water. It is hoped that the redirection of water into aquifers will relieve future flooding and drought situations.

Regulations will be enforced and controlled by new permits required by the New Jersey Department of Environmental Protection. Public education about the new regulations, non-point source pollution and how each citizen can play an active role in maintaining clean, accessible water will be emphasized.

The Watershed Watch Network is an umbrella organization of volunteer monitoring programs for stormwater regulations and other programs. Due to the limited resources of agencies, volunteers can help insure a program's success.

A task force was also established in 2004 to address pollution and hazardous waste in urban areas of the state. While the focus of many of the environmental regulations implemented during this time period were aimed at open space, the mission of this group was to make sure that minorities, low-income and other residents living in urban areas were being protected from environmental dangers, as well.

Ozone and fine particles causing pollution were also addressed. It is estimated that meeting new federal pollution regulations would eliminate 40,000 cases of asthma in New Jersey each year.[69] Regulations are being drawn up to bring pollution producing industries in line with federal guidelines.

Tighter emission controls have been suggested to reduce the impact vehicles have on our environment. Cars cause more than forty percent of the air pollution in New Jersey and spew out more than eighty percent of the airborne carcinogens.[70] Improving inspections for diesel vehicles and tighter restrictions against idling buses and trucks will also help.

Through a cooperative effort between the Department of Environmental Protection and the Bureau of Public Utilities, over three million dollars was donated to plant over five thousand trees in urban areas. The goal was to reduce hotter temperatures in urban areas, which is known as the "Heat Island effect." Additionally, the trees will reduce air pollution, increase property values and provide a better quality of life for residents in those areas.

One of the greatest steps toward environmental education was the development of the "I-Map" – an interactive map that can be updated digitally and accessed in "real-time" by anyone with a computer. The map displays waterways, greenbelts, counties and various environmental criteria, which can be selected and displayed in layers. The map has zoom controls that will permit displays ranging from an overview of the entire state right up to a close-up on a resident's house. Areas of special concern or study can easily be identified. As new data and information are added to databases, this information can easily be retrieved and displayed.

Numerous grants are provided to municipalities and environmental groups by the Department of Environmental Protection, on a matching funds basis, to provide education and develop outreach programs that benefit the public and the environment. Volunteers are always needed to research, write and implement these grants.

Why preserve open space and conserve land? Development of land can be a lengthy process whereas conservation is a much quicker return on the dollar for the land and it provides tax benefits as well. Here are some other possible benefits of conservation:

- tax stabilization — no increased demand for new schools, first aid and police services and road infrastructure
- pristine land can serve as habitat for threatened and endangered species
- greenbelts for passive or active recreation
- valuable farms can be saved and receive funding for upgrades and needed equipment
- preservation of natural resources
- scenic views
- historic preservation

Each year, the state Green Acres Program receives approximately one hundred and fifteen million dollars from the Garden State Preservation Trust. Fifty percent of that is used for direct land purchase, forty percent for matching grants and loans to municipalities and counties, and the remaining ten percent to matching grants for non-profit trusts.

The Natural Lands Trust Program was established in 1997 after voters approved a dedicated tax to purchase environmentally sensitive open spaces. As of 2009, Ocean County, NJ, has preserved 4,536 acres through the Natural Lands Trust Program.

Non-profit agencies, such as the Trust for Public Land, help identify land to be conserved, locate funds to aid in preservation and assist in raising funds. The Trust for Public Land does not generally provide grants, but can aid in applying for them.

Preserving farmland is also important. The Farmland Preservation Program offers farmers the opportunity to permanently preserve their land while retaining title to the land, the ability to continue farming it and payment for their easement consideration. Payment is based on the difference between the farmland tax assessed value of the land and what the land value would be if it were to be fully developed.

This money can be used to upgrade farm equipment, purchase needed supplies, reduce debt or provide retirement savings. In addition to the funding they receive, landowners are also eligible to apply for cost-sharing grants for soil and water conservation projects. They receive limited protection from government eminent domain acquisition, public and private nuisances and emergency restrictions on water and energy supplies.

Statewide, six hundred and sixty-eight farms covering approximately 90,000 acres have been preserved. Between 1995 and 2000, farm acreage decreased from 1.8 million acres to 800,000 acres. The number of farms decreased during this time period from 26,900 to only 8,600, statewide.

The Landowner Incentive Program (LIP) is administered through the Fish and Wildlife Division of the New Jersey Department of Environmental Protection's Endangered Species Program.

Since many endangered and threatened species exist on privately owned land, the Department of Environmental Protection is partnering with individual landowners to help protect the habitat of these species.

Critically sensitive areas have been mapped out and owners of land in these targeted areas can work with a Department of Environmental Protection biologist to submit a proposal to properly maintain the necessary habitat for these species.

Landowners whose proposals are accepted will sign a contract with the Department of Environmental Protection to allow biologists onto the site for periodic checks, will provide twenty-five percent of the expenses for maintaining the site on a cost share basis with Department of Environmental Protection and must participate for a minimum of five years.

What does all of this mean to Colliers Mills? Well, land that is preserved and adjacent to Colliers Mills provides an additional greenway of contiguous land for wildlife. Endangered and threatened species may reside in Colliers Mills because of proximity to food, shelter or other attractive conditions in adjacent land. Providing a buffer also helps to protect the ecosystems in Colliers Mills.

Since the land is already preserved and unable to be sold to developers, when landowners or their estates look to sell the land, Colliers Mills is a viable option as a purchaser. And lastly, income from the Farmland Preservation Program can benefit Colliers Mills as well. In the northwest corner of Colliers Mills, several acres are farmed under this program, providing revenue to the wildlife management area.

The future of greenbelts such as Colliers Mills, the potability of drinking water from the aquifers that flow beneath the pines – and even our own futures – depend on the decisions that each of us makes every day.

Colliers Mills Today

Colliers Mills has come full circle. Its original uses of hunting and fishing support the wildlife management area today. Numerous sports activities – organized and individual – take place there every day.

Today, Colliers Mills consists of 12,652 acres, with acres occasionally being added, as neighboring landowners donate their property. It is one of one hundred and eighteen wildlife management areas in the state. These areas make up forty-four percent of state owned land.

They fall under the jurisdiction of the Division of Fish and Wildlife of the New Jersey Department of Environmental Protection. The NJDEP is responsible for issuing permits, enforcing regulations and patrolling the park. Following are a sample of some of the uses.

Orienteering

This sport originated in Scandinavia in the nineteenth century as a military training exercise. By 1919, it had evolved into a competitive sport in Sweden.[71] It was brought to the United States by Bjorn Kjellstrom in 1946.

Orienteering basically consists of a designed course in the woods dotted with "control points" – small flags with numbers of the station on them. Course maps are given to participants who try to find all of the control points on their trail by reading map symbols such as a clearing, lake, tall stand of trees or other symbols. Usually the control point contains something to mark the course map with to prove the person found the control – such as a paper punch with a unique symbol on it.

There may be several trails associated with an orienteering event. For example, seven trails may be used in a particular course, ranging from beginning to difficult. Beginners have less control points to find, the controls are in more accessible areas and the symbols have written explanations on them. As the trails increase in difficulty, only symbols appear on the maps.

Orienteering can be both fun and challenging. Many see the trails as a challenge to find all of the control points; more advanced competitors race through the trail, hoping not only to find all of the controls, but also to do so in the shortest amount of time.

Regardless of the difficulty of the trail chosen, orienteering is a great way to find new trails, discover unknown habitat and test your sense of direction in the woods. Organized orienteering events require everyone to sign in and document the time you embark and the trail that you have chosen. Should you get lost and not return in an appropriate time frame, organizers will search for you. Orienteering is a great way for someone to learn his or her way around unmarked trails safely, without the fear of getting lost.

My first orienteering event was held in Colliers Mills. I had walked and driven through most of the area by this time, yet I discovered quite a few new areas while completing my map. Orienteering also sharpens your senses and observation skills. When walking through an area that I was familiar with alongside one of the many lakes, I noticed a board had been placed across a small stream. The board had not been affected by the elements and I knew I had not seen it there before, so I correctly surmised that it had been placed there by the orienteering organizers. By crossing it, I found my next control point.

Hunting

All persons ten years of age and older must have a valid hunting license. Those twelve and older need a trapping license in order to trap. Licenses must be openly displayed on outer clothing and available to show to any person requesting to see it.

Those who own farmland tax assessed property (minimum of five acres and five hundred dollars of gross income per year required) may hunt, trap and fish on their property without a license or valid rifle permit. This only applies, however, to the immediate family members of the owner and not anyone else who wishes to hunt on the land.

New Jersey law mandates that anyone applying to hunt with a rifle, bow or shotgun must complete a hunter education course. The course is available on home video, there is a homework assignment to complete and testing is done at approved facilities before a license can be issued.

Disabled veterans, as determined by the United States Department of Veteran Affairs, are eligible to receive a free permit for the permit bow season and one free firearm permit for either the permit shotgun or permit muzzleloader season. The hunter education course is still required and the permit must be obtained directly from the Division of Fish and Wildlife office.

A select number of permits are issued each year for beaver, otter, turkey, falcon, coyote, red and gray fox, and black bear. There are three permit seasons for white-tailed deer in order to manage the population. Each permit is only good for the season issued.

If you accidentally kill a deer with your vehicle and wish to possess the deer for meat consumption purposes only, you are required to obtain a free permit from the police department or division law enforcement agency. The permit is good for ninety days and does not allow the driver to take possession of the antlers.[72]

Deer hunting is also permitted in county and state parks under a strict set of regulations that may change per season. It is always best to obtain the latest requirements before applying for a permit.

All hunters must wear a cap or outer garment of daylight fluorescent orange visible from all sides while hunting deer, bear, rabbit, hare, fox, railbirds, game birds and squirrel.

Wildlife management areas such as Colliers Mills have additional sets of regulations, which include prohibition of hunting woodchucks with rifles, hunting after 9PM or before 5AM without special approval, and the use of waterfowl blinds.

Swimming

On the eastern shore of Lake Success, there is an area absent of vegetation where the sandy soil is visible. If you stand in that spot on a clear sunny July afternoon and squint your eyes, you can almost see heads bobbing in the water and the laughter of children chasing each other across the sand. With a decent wind current, the waves lap at the sand and you can feel yourself transported back in time when the lakes of Colliers Mills beckoned as a resort area.

Some of the older residents of neighboring New Egypt remember the days when their fathers would come home from work and the family would pile up in the car and take an evening dip in Colliers Mills Lake to cool off. From the sepia toned photographs I have viewed, it was a popular family activity in those humid days before air conditioning.

However, swimming is a prohibited activity in Colliers Mills today.

Dog Training and Exercise

Exercise and dog training is permitted in designated areas only from May 1st to August 31st and anywhere else during other times with the exception of the Friday before the opening day of the regular small game season. Dogs must be properly licensed.

Waterfowl

Numerous waterfowl abound in Colliers Mills. Since hunters have daily limits, it behooves them to learn how to quickly identify different species. Waterfowl can be distinguished by size, shape, plumage patterns and coloration, behavior, calls and habitat.

Flock maneuvers also help identify species. For example, mallards and pintails fly in loose groups; teal and shovelers move in tight bunches. In flight, their silhouettes also provide clues.

Calls are also important. Not all ducks quack, contrary to popular belief. Some grunt, whistle or squeal. Male ducks, known as drakes, will lose their bright plumage after mating and may resemble females. Most ducks will shed their body feathers twice a year.

Members of waterfowl associations use Colliers Mills to train their dogs. Competitions are held here throughout the year. Please check with the association chapter you are interested in for dates and more specific information.

The New Jersey Waterfowlers Association is a statewide, nonprofit organization. It has four main goals: represent all waterfowlers in a unified voice to agencies such as the Division of Fish and Wildlife, educate the public on the value of wetlands, offer educational programs and training to the waterfowler about his sport, and promote waterfowl nesting habitat and research.[73]

Some ongoing projects of the association include decoy carving, building wood duck nesting boxes, research on the black duck population and the neck banding of Canada geese.

Fishing

Colliers Mills' numerous streams, ponds and lakes offer an abundant variety of fish for those who enjoy the sport. Fishermen are seen on a daily basis, casting their lines into the water or teaching the youngsters how to fish.

Following is a list of species found in the New Jersey Pine Barrens:[74]

- American Eel (*Anguilla rostrata*)
- Redfin (Grass) Pickerel (*Esoc americanus*)
- Chain Pickerel (*Esox Niger*)
- Eastern Mudminnow (*Umbra pygmaea*)
- Golden Shiner (*Notemigonus crysoleuces*)
- Creek Chubsucker (*Erimyzon oblongus*)
- Yellow Bullhead (*Ictalurus natalis*)
- Brown Bullhead (*Ictalurus nebulosus*)
- Tadpole Madtom (*Noturus gyrinus*)
- Pirate Perch (*Aphredoderus sayanus*)
- Mud Sunfish (*Acantharchus pomotis*)
- Blackbanded Sunfish (*Enneacanthus chaetodon*)
- Banded Sunfish (*Enneacanthus obesus*)
- Pumpkinseed (*Lepomis gibbosus*)
- Swamp Darter (*Etheostoma fusiforme*)
- Tassellated Darter (*Etheostoma olmstedi*)
- Yellow Perch (*Perca flavescens*)

Boating

Vehicles used to transport boats to and from wildlife management areas in the state are required to have a boat ramp maintenance permit affixed to the lower corner of the driver's side rear window. Drivers age seventy and older are not required to purchase these permits but must affix proof of age to the driver's side rear window.

Electric motors are allowed on freshwater areas. Manually controlled boats such as rowboats and canoes are permitted on water throughout Colliers Mills. The deep clean waters of most of Colliers Mills lakes make this a beautiful and easily navigable place to canoe. The wildlife management area is home to almost one hundred and fifty acres of water surface.

Horseback Riding

Horseback riding is permitted on designated trails throughout Colliers Mills with a permit from the Division of Fish and Wildlife. The permit must be displayed on outer clothing while riding. Permits can be obtained for twenty-five dollars by calling 609.259.2132.

The extensive range of trails is best seen on horseback in order to cover more ground and reach areas inaccessible by car. Many of the dirt trails are too narrow to permit vehicles, allowing horseback riding without fear of horses being spooked by passing vehicles.

Numerous horse farms surround Colliers Mills, particularly on the northwest side in Plumsted Township. There are many stalls available for private boarding and some farms offer horse rentals for those that do not have their own.

Ranges

When you enter Colliers Mills through the main entrance off Hawkin Road and follow the dirt road to a fork, there will be a number of ranges to the left. The area is marked with a sign. The ranges are all surrounded by woods, which help absorb the sound.

Muzzle loading rifles, shotguns – buckshot or slugs – and .22 rim fire are permitted at the ranges here. Pistols and center fire is not allowed. Only paper targets can be used.

According to posted regulations: "The range area is open to licensed hunters and their guests only. At least one member of each group must have a current New Jersey hunting license in their possession. Hunter education classes are given first priority over those using the range area. Infraction of these regulations will be cause for expulsion from this range and or fines which could lead to license revocation."

Shotgun Training Area

The sign at the entrance reads, "This is your range. Leave your range as good as or better than you found it" and people do. In all the times that I have been to Colliers Mills, I have always found the ranges to be clean and well kept. Others may litter, but those paying for licenses and using Colliers Mills to practice seem to have respect for the area.

In the shotgun training area, only clay birds or paper pattern boards are permitted. Slugs and buckshot are not allowed. Only fine shot – smaller than number four lead or number T steel ammunition – is permitted here. Eye and ear protection must be worn.

The shotgun training area is open to licensed hunters and their guests only. At least one member of each group must have a current New Jersey hunting license in their possession. Hunter education classes are given first priority over those using the shotgun area.

Miscellaneous Vehicles

All terrain vehicles, or ATVs, are strictly prohibited from Colliers Mills and all other wildlife management areas in the state. Violation of this law is frequent and offenders are summonsed on an almost daily basis in Colliers Mills.

Those who enjoy riding these vehicles do not realize the destruction of trails and woodland that these vehicles cause. The loud noise emitted from them frightens wildlife and the dust kicked up by their wheels contributes to poor visibility. Many a rider has been injured or killed when accidentally wandering onto a road in front of a motor vehicle that couldn't stop in time or driving into a gully or across uneven terrain. Besides ATVs, the use of dog sleds, dog carts, trail bikes, off road vehicles and snowmobiles are also prohibited.

Archery

Archery is the art of shooting with a bow and arrow. These are probably one of the first refined weapons used by man. Archery became an official sport in England in 1673. The oldest, continuous archery tournament is the Ancient Scorton Arrow Contest, held in England.

In America, the first archery organization was the National Archery Association, created in 1879.[75] Although competitions occasionally took place, archery only became an official sport in the Olympics in 1972.

There are four main types of archery: field archery (using bows without sights), flight shooting (for distance), crossbow (using a crossbow instead of bow and arrow) and target shooting (scoring points with number of arrows aimed at target's center).

Colliers Mills permits bow and field tipped arrows only. No broadheads are allowed. Only paper, foam and straw targets may be used. The archery area is open to licensed hunters and their guests only. The archery area is located off the same road as the ranges, just a short distance down from the shotgun training area. At least one member of each group must have a current New Jersey hunting license in their possession. Hunter education classes are given first priority over those using the archery area.

Law Enforcement Training Center – Range Road

When you come in the main entrance of Colliers Mills and cross over the bridge that divides Colliers Mills Pond from Turnmill Pond, you'll pass a gated entrance on your right. That road leads to a restricted area where law enforcement officers conduct various training activities. At times, if a lot of activity is anticipated, you may find the gate open, however, public access is not permitted. It is best not to enter that area by foot, either, as you don't know what activities may be taking place and you don't want to put yourself or any of the officers at risk.

Astronomy

Stars can readily be seen in this area because of the scarcity of streetlights and the fairly open spaces. But when unusual phenomenon crosses the sky, such as a distant planet, moon or comet, astronomy clubs come to Colliers Mills.

The tremendous stretch of open space, devoid of any artificial light, creates an ideal habitat for those who study the stars. However, since the wildlife management area is closed to the public after dark, permission must be arranged in advance. But the Division of Fish and Wildlife is always glad to accommodate those on a cosmic mission.

Airfield

Near the law enforcement training center is an airstrip/runaway that was built years ago for the New Jersey Fire Service, in the event they needed to land a plane in this area. The runaway is seldom used, and along with Emson's racetrack, is one of the best-kept secrets in Colliers Mills.

Dumping

Dumping is a large problem in Collier's Mills. Because of its seclusion, people feel that they can haul large amounts of refuse into the wildlife area without being seen. One of the biggest problems is the dumping of toxic or hazardous materials, such as paint cans, used oil and air conditioners containing freon.

There is no easy solution to the problem. Recycling centers that accept hazardous material may charge a fee, only permit disposal during certain time periods and may be some distance from the dumper's home. While most people are conscientious enough to dispose of these materials properly or pay someone else to do it, human nature dictates that there will always be some that will choose the easy – and often illegal – way out.

Obviously, large or hazardous materials need to be taken to the proper facilities. There is always the hazard of these materials being ingested by wildlife. Antifreeze, which is highly toxic to animals, has a sweet odor that often attracts animals to its presence. Even the proper disposal of smaller items that may be consumed or used can present a disposal problem.

Back in 1987, the Department of Environmental Protection (DEP) attempted to put 15,000 drums of radium-contaminated soil in Colliers Mills. The soil came from the backyards of residents living in Montclair, Glen Ridge and West Orange.

The plan was thwarted by the combined efforts of local citizens and politicians who did not want to see the wildlife management area negatively impacted in this way. I tell the full story of the origin of the radon and the battle to prevent its dumping, in my second book, *Voices in the Pines: True Stories from the New Jersey Barrens.* Interviews conducted with the folks involved, plus excerpts from public documents never printed publicly before, are contained here.

It is the incredible story of governmental agencies attempting to act in violation of their own laws, and how the public and certain elected officials decided they were going to stand up to them and not allow Colliers Mills to be a dumping ground.

Conservation Officers

The fifty member force of the Division of Fish and Wildlife's Conservation Office is responsible for enforcing laws anywhere that wildlife can be taken or possessed. Primarily, they are seen in public parks and wildlife management areas, but their jurisdiction does not end there.

Conservation officers are law enforcement officers employed by the State of New Jersey, just like state park rangers and state troopers. However, conservation officers belong to the DEP. State troopers work for the Department of Law and Public Safety. Park rangers are part of the Division of Parks and Forestry, another division of the Department of Environmental Protection.

They wear green and gray uniforms and are sometimes referred to as "game wardens". While they have full police authority, their primary mission focuses on wildlife.

Most days are spent patrolling the parks, forests and wildlife areas they are assigned to. Job responsibilities are varied and can include following up on wildlife abuse calls, writing summonses, testifying in court, checking hunting licenses and chasing down illegally operated ATVs.

How do you become a conservation officer? First, you must have a bachelor degree in biology, natural resource management or a related field. You must have at least eighteen credit hours in wildlife science or fisheries. After applying, if you score high enough on the Civil Service entrance exam, you may be invited to join the force.

Next, you will receive one hundred and forty-two hours of wildlife law enforcement instruction from the Bureau of Law Enforcement and attend five months of police academy training.

After that, you will learn on the job for a year with an experienced conservation officer. Conservation officers must keep up-to-date, physically fit and able to fully serve at all times. Four times a year, officers are required to re-qualify with the weapon used in the field. You must also take ongoing courses in first aid, self-defense and search and seizure.

Conservation officers are required to be on call twenty-four hours a day so you must live in the county for which you are hired to work. Generally, two officers are assigned per county. The conservation officers for Colliers Mills work out of the Central Regional Office in the Assunpink Wildlife Refuge, a few miles to the north of Colliers Mills.

Being a conservation officer may look glamorous, but it is a physically demanding job where your life is put on the line every day. An average of 5,000 summonses are written agency-wide each year. Seven conservation officers have died in the line of duty in New Jersey. Because you are most busy during the height of the hunting season, you have little free time to enjoy the areas you protect each day.

But the job is rewarding, knowing that you are helping maintain wildlife areas for future generations. And the hundreds of thousands of dollars that are collected in fines are put into the Hunter and Angler Fund, which pay for fish and wildlife conservation.[76]

Hiking

On the northern end of Colliers Mills, located off Route 528 and east of Hawkin Road, you will find Stump Tavern Road. If you turn onto this paved road, past the developments, you will see a dirt road. If you follow this road, about a quarter mile in is a hill, with sand and tree roots exposed on the right hand side. A smaller dirt road crosses east to west by that hill.

The climb to the top is a short one as the slope of the hill steeps dramatically. The road you were on, if you were traveling north, had begun to climb gradually in altitude. As you move upward, deep gullies have worn into the dirt from rainfall erosion. The scraggly roots of a pine tree protrude from the side.

Once you reach the top, the sights will astound you. As you look westward, all you can see are treetops. In the near distance is another hill about the same height as the one you are standing on. This is referred to as the "stone hills" of Plumsted and it was a favorite spot of naturalist Elizabeth Meirs Morgan. These hills are approximately two hundred and twenty-five feet above sea level.

The horizon appears far off in the distance. A sunset viewed from this hill is exquisite. As you drink in the tranquility of the scenery around you, it is easy to imagine yourself as one of the earlier villagers, a cranberry picker from Emson's time or Switlik himself.

You can imagine the sense of freedom that Amelia Earhart must have felt as she drifted downward in her parachute jump that day. From this perspective, no man-made inventions are visible and you could just as well be a Lenape on his way home from a hunt.

As you climb down from the hill, your view of Colliers Mills will never quite be the same.

You get back in your car and continue north until another dirt road crosses east to west. You turn east and the road takes many twists and turns as it snakes southeast. During one of these turns, the ground will climb a bit to your left. Park your car, as you walk towards the left, the ground gradually climbs upward. This is a much more gradual climb than the last and will take you longer as you travel more ground. Continue following the narrow trails until you reach the top.

You are now standing roughly the same height above sea level as before. Only this time, the perspective is quite different. If you face east, south or west, the view is mainly the tops of pine trees and taller oaks. But as you turn to face north, you see a yellow and blue roller coaster in the distance. You may catch a glimpse of other rides if the visibility is good. You are looking at Six Flags Great Adventure, an amusement park built on land purchased from Switlik in the early 70's.

You may also see utility lines snaking along Route 537 and cellular towers for phone transmission. Suddenly, that feeling of reliving the past that you experienced on the other hill is gone. Here, the old mixes with the new; nature meshes with technology.

Still, the view is quite breathtaking and certainly not something you see every day in the mainly flat terrain of Ocean County. As you head back down, you have been given even more to think about.

Is change always good – or even desirable? What is the price we pay for our technological advancements? Would we put on the brakes or slow down if we knew then what we know today?

The wonder of wildlife management areas such as Colliers Mills is that we can come here to examine our thoughts, connect with our past and enjoy various activities. Ephraim Emson and Amelia Earhart stood on the threshold of time as we do today.

What does the future hold for us and for areas like Colliers Mills?

As you have seen, Colliers Mills offers activities for both the passive and active recreationist. Its sugar sand trails allow hunters and photographers alike the opportunity to capture wildlife in their natural environment. Fathers teach their sons to fish in the many lakes that they themselves learned in, many years before, from their own fathers.

It has the outside appearance of a land untouched by time, but yet we have seen the ghosts of towns and villages that sprung up here, only to return to dust and sand. Its echoes of the past whisper the secrets of Colliers Mills through the pines.

As Stanley Switlik said over fifty years ago as he stood on the shore of Success Lake, "May the public...always enjoy this place."

Appendix A

Threatened and Endangered Plants of the New Jersey Pinelands

The fifty-four threatened and endangered plants of the New Jersey Pinelands are afforded special protection under the Pinelands Comprehensive Management Plan. This plan essentially prohibits development activities anywhere that may cause adverse impact on the survival of local populations of these species.[77]

Common name:	Botantical name:
Sensitive-joint vetch, Virginia jointvetch	*Aeschynomene virginica*
Red milkweed	*Asclepias rubra*
Pine Barrens reedgrass; Pine Barren sandreed	*Calamovilfa brevipilis*
Barratt's Sedge	*Carex barrattii*
Spreading pogonia; Rosebud orchid	*Cleistes divaricata*
Broom Crowberry	*Corema conradii*
Rose-colored tickseed; pink tickseed	*Coreopsis rosea*
Rushfoil; Willdenow's croton	*Croton willdenowii*
Stiff tick trefoil; Pine Barren ticktrefoil	*Desmodium strictum*
Hirst's panic grass	*Dichanthelium hirstii*
Knotted spike rush; jointed spikesedge	*Eleocharis equisetoides*
Resinous boneset; Pine Barren thoroughwort	*Eupatorium resinosum*
Pine Barrens gentian	*Gentiana autumnalis*
Swamp pink	*Helonias bullata*
New Jersey rush	*Juncus caesariensis*
Lily-leaved twayblade; brown widelip orchid	*Liparis liliifolia*
Loesel's twayblade; yellow widelip orchid	*Liparis loeselii*
Southern twayblade	*Listera australis*
Boykin's lobelia	*Lobelia boykinii*
Canby's lobelia	*Lobelia canbyi*
Hairy ludwigia; spindleroot	*Ludwigia hirtella*
Linear-leaved ludwigia; narrowleaf primrose-willow	*Ludwigia linearis*

Climbing fern; American climbing fern	*Lygodium palmatum*
Torrey's muhly; New Jersey muhly	*Muhlenbergia torreyana*
Yellow asphodel	*Narthecium americanum*
Floating heart; little floatingheart	*Nymphoides cordata*
Narrow panic grass; maidencane	*Panicum hemitomon*
Sickle-leaved golden aster; sickleleaf silkgrass	*Pityopsis falcate*
American mistletoe; oak mistletoe	*Phoradendron leucarpum*
Yellow-fringed orchid	*Platanthera ciliaris*
Crested yellow orchid	*Platanthera cristata*
Southern yellow orchid; yellow fringeless orchid	*Platanthera integra*
Maryland milkwort	*Polygala mariana*
Slender rattlesnake root	*Prenanthes autumnalis*
Awned meadow beauty; awnpetal meadowbeauty	*Rhexia aristosa*
Capitate beakrush; bunched beaksedge	*Rhynchospora cephalantha*
Slender beaked rush; narrowfruit horned beaksedge	*Rhynchospora inundata*
Knieskern's beaked rush; Knieskern's beaksedge	*Rhynchospora knieskernii*
Curly grass fern; little curlygrass fern	*Schizaea pusilla*
Chaffseed	*Schwalbea Americana*
Long's bulrush	*Scirpus longii*
Slender nut rush	*Scleria minor*
Reticulated nut rush; netted nutrush	*Scleria reticularis*
Sclerolepis; pink bogbutton	*Sclerolepis uniflora*
Wand-like goldenrod; wand goldenrod	*Solidago stricta*
Little ladies'-tresses	*Spiranthes tuberosa*
Pickering's morning glory; Pickering's dawnflower	*Stylisma pickeringii*
Silvery aster; Eastern silver aster	*Symphyotrichum concolor*
False asphodel; coastal false asphodel	*Tofieldia racemosa*
Humped bladderwort	*Utricularia gibba*
White-flowered bladderwort; Piedmont bladderwort	*Utricularia olivacea*

Purple bladderwort; Eastern purple bladderwort	*Utricularia purpurea*
Reclined bladderwort; lavender bladderwort	*Utricularia resupinata*
Yellow-eyed grass; Carolina yelloweyed grass	*Xyris caroliniana*

Appendix B

Threatened and Endangered Animals of the New Jersey Pinelands

The forty-four animal species listed below are classified as threatened or endangered by the New Jersey Division of Fish and Wildlife, Endangered and Nongame Species Program, and are known to occur within the Pinelands National Reserve. This list does not include threatened and endangered marine mammals or sea turtles that may occur in backbays or other estuarine waters within the Pinelands National Reserve.[78]

Common Name	Botanical Name	Status*
Birds		
Cooper's Hawk	*Accipiter cooperii*	T
Northern groshawk	*Accipiter gentilis*	E
Henslow's sparrow	*Ammodramus henslowii*	E
Grasshopper sparrow	*Ammodramus savannarum*	T
Short-eared owl	*Asio flammeus*	T-B
Long-eared owl	*Asio otus*	T
Upland sandpiper	*Batramia longicauda*	E
Red-shouldered hawk	*Buteo lineatus*	E-B,T-NB
American bittern	*Botaurus lentiginosos*	E
Piping plover	*Charadrius melodus*	E, FT
Northern harrier	*Circus cyaneus*	E-B
Sedge wren	*Cistothorus platensis*	E
Bobolink	*Dolichonyx-oryzivorus*	T
Peregrine falcon	*Falco peregrinus*	E
Bald eagle	*Haliaeetus leucocephalus*	E, FT
Loggerhead shrike	*Lanius ludovicianus*	E
Black rail	*Laterallus jamaicensis*	T
Red-headed woodpecker	*Melanerpes erthrocephalus*	T
Black-crowned night heron	*Nycticorax nycticorax*	T
Yellow-crowned night heron	*Nyctanassa violaceus*	T

Osprey	*Pandion haliaetus*	T
Savannah sparrow	*Passerculus sandwichensis*	T
Pied-billed grebe	*Podilymbus podiceps*	E-B
Vesper sparrow	*Pooecetes gramineus*	E
Black skimmer	*Rynchops niger*	E
Least tern	*Sterna antillarum*	E
Roseate tern	*Sterna dougallii*	E, FE
Barred owl	*Strix varia*	T

Reptiles

Wood turtle	*Clemmys insculpta*	T
Bog turtle	*Clemmys muhlenbergii*	E, FT
Timber rattlesnake	*Crotalus horridus*	E
Corn snake	*Elaphe guttata*	E
Northern pine snake	*Pituophis m. melanoleucus*	T

Amphibians

Blue-spotted salamander	*Ambystoma laterale*	E
Eastern tiger salamander	*Ambystoma tigrinum*	E
Pine Barrens treefrog	*Hyla andersonii*	T
Southern grey treefrog	*Hyla chrysocelis*	E
Eastern mud turtle	*Pseudotriton montanus*	T

Mammals

| Bobcat | *Lynx rufus* | E |

Invertebrates

Arogos skipper (butterfly)	*Atrytone arogos arogos*	E
Northeastern beach tiger beetle	*Cincindela dorsalis dorsalis*	E, FT
Silver-bordered fritillary (butterfly)	*Bolaria selene myrina*	T
Frosted Elfin (butterfly)	*Callophrys irus*	T

*Status legend:

E	Endangered
T	Threatened
FT	Federally threatened
FE	Federally endangered
B	Breeding populations only
NB	Non-breeding populations only

Appendix C

Torrey Botanical Society Field Trip Sightings List

A field trip by the Torrey Botanical Society was led by field botantist Linda Kelly through Colliers Mills on July 28, 2001. Present on the tour were Karl Anderson, Patrick Cooney and Dr. William F. Standaert, who served as recording secretary for the trip.

The list that follows is a partial list of some of the plants encountered during that trip, and in no way, suggests a complete list of the abundant flora found in Colliers Mills. I have included it here to give a sample of variety of plant species that can be found in this wildlife management area.

Common Name	Botanical Name
Trees	
Red Maple	*Acer rubrum*
Silver Maple	*Acer saccharinum*
Eastern Serviceberry	*Amelanchier canadensis*
Gray Birch	*Betula populifolia*
Chinese Chestnut	*Castanea mollissima*
Hackberry	*Celtis occidentalis*
Atlantic White Cedar	*Chamaecyparis thyoides*
Black Walnut	*Juglans nigra*
Eastern Red-cedar	*Juniperus virginiana*
White Mulberry	*Morus alba*
Sour Gum	*Nyssa sylvatica*
Pitch Pine	*Pinus rigida*
Black Cherry	*Prunus serotina*
White Oak	*Quercus alba*
Blackjack Oak	*Quercus marilandica*

Chestnut Oak	*Quercus prinus*
Black Oak	*Quercus velutina*
Black Locust	*Robinia pseudoacacia*
Black Willow	*Salix sp.*
Sassafras	*Sassafras albidum*

Shrubs

Buttonbush	*Cephalanthus occidentalis*
Leatherleaf	*Chamaedaphne calyculata* (common)
Sweet Pepperbush	*Clethra alnifolia*
Swamp Loosestrife	*Decodon verticillatus*
Fetterbush	*Eubotrys racemosa*
Eastern Teaberry	*Gaultheria procumbens* (some)
Black Huckleberry	*Gaylussacia baccata*
Dwarf Huckleberry	*Gaylussacia dumosa var.* (few)
Dangleberry	*Gaylussacia frondosa*
Golden Heather	*Hudsonia ericoides*
St. Andrew's Cross	*Hypericum stragulum* (common)
Inkberry	*Ilex glabra*
Sheep Laurel	*Kalmia angustifolia*
Mountain Laurel	*Kalmia latifolia*
Sand-myrtle	*Leiophyllum buxifolium*
Maleberry	*Lyonia ligustrina*
Staggerbush	*Lyonia mariana*
Bayberry	*Myrica pensylvanica*
Scrub Oak	*Quercus ilicifolia* (some)
Swamp Azalea	*Rhododendron viscosum*
Multiflora Rose	*Rosa multiflora* (few, entrance area)
Sand Blackberry	*Rubus cuneifolius* (few)
Bog Dewberry	*Rubus hispidus*
Black Raspberry	*Rubus occidentalis*
Blackberry	*Rubus sp.*
Common Elderberry	*Sambucus canadensis*

Steeplebush	*Spiraea tomentosa*
Lilac	*Syringa vulgaris*
Lowbush Blueberry	*Vaccinium angustifolium*
Highbush Blueberry	*Vaccinium corymbosum*
Cranberry	*Vaccinium macrocarpon*

Vines

Groundnut	*Apios americana*
Common Dodder	*Cuscuta gronovii*
Dodder	*Cuscuta sp.*
Japanese Hop	*Humulus japonicus*
Japanese Honeysuckle	*Lonicera japonica*
Climbing Hempvine	*Mikania scandens*
Virginia Creeper	*Parthenocissus quinquefolia*
Glaucous Greenbrier	*Smilax glauca*
Common Greenbrier	*Smilax rotundifolia*
Poison Ivy	*Toxicodendron radicans*
Summer Grape	*Vitis aestivalis*

Herbs

Three-seeded Mercury	*Acalypha rhomboidea*
Yarrow	*Achillea millefolium ssp. lanulosa*
Wild Garlic	*Allium vineale*
Common Ragweed	*Ambrosia artemisiifolia*
Indian Hemp	*Apocynum cannabinum*
Pine Barren Sandwort	*Arenaria caroliniana*
Mugwort	*Artemisia vulgaris*
Swamp Milkweed	*Asclepias incarnata*
Common Milkweed	*Asclepias syriaca*
Butterfly Milkweed	*Asclepias tuberosa*
Twining Screwstem	*Bartonia paniculata*
Yellow Screwstem	*Bartonia virginica*

Hoary Alyssum	*Berteroa incana*
False Nettle	*Boehmeria cylindrica*
Watershield	*Brasenia schreberi*
Spotted Knapweed	*Centaurea maculosa*
Lamb's-quarters	*Chenopodium album*
Spotted Wintergreen	*Chimaphila maculata*
Maryland Goldenaster	*Chrysopsis mariana*
Field Thistle	*Cirsium discolor*
Asiatic Dayflower	*Commelina communis*
Lily of the Valley	*Convallaria majalis*
Crown Vetch	*Coronilla varia*
Glandular Croton	*Croton glandulosus*
Wild Carrot	*Daucus carota*
Buttonweed	*Diodia teres*
Thread-leaved Sundew	*Drosera filiformis*
Spatulate-leaved Sundew	*Drosera intermedia*
Round-leaved Sundew	*Drosera rotundifolia*
Lesser Daisy Fleabane	*Erigeron strigosus*
Hyssop-leaved Thoroughwort	*Eupatorium hyssopifolium*
Sweetscented Joe-Pye Weed	*Eupatorium purpureum*
White Snakeroot	*Eupatorium rugosum*
Eyebane	*Euphorbia nutans*
Flat-top Goldenrod	*Euthamia graminifolia*
Slender Goldenrod	*Euthamia tenuifolia var.*
Virginia Strawberry	*Fragaria virginiana*
Slender Cottonweed	*Froelichia gracilis*
Hairy Bedstraw	*Galium pilosum*
Virginia Stickseed	*Hackelia virginiana*
Glaucous King Devil	*Hieracium piloselloides*
Canadian St. Johnswort	*Hypericum canadense*
Orangegrass	*Hypericum gentianoides*
Common St. Johnswort	*Hypericum perforatum*
Cat's-ear	*Hypochoeris radicata*
Jewelweed	*Impatiens capensis*

Sheep's-bit	*Jasione montana*
Redroot	*Lachnanthes caroliniana*
Oblong-fruited Pinweed	*Lechea racemulosa*
Horehound Motherwort	*Leonurus marrubiastrum*
Peppergrass	*Lepidium virginicum*
Silky Lespedeza	*Lespedeza cuneata*
Blue Toadflax	*Linaria canadensis*
Ridged Yellow Flax	*Linum striatum*
Nuttall's Lobelia	*Lobelia nuttallii*
Birdfoot Trefoil	*Lotus corniculatus*
Virginia Water Horehound?	*Lycopus sp. (virginicus?)*
Purple Loosestrife	*Lythrum salicaria*
Cow-wheat	*Melampyrum lineare*
Wild Bergamot	*Monarda fistulosa*
Bullhead Pond-lily	*Nuphar variegata*
White Waterlily	*Nymphaea odorata*
Evening-primrose	*Oenothera biennis*
Yellow Woodsorrel	*Oxalis stricta*
Arrow Arum	*Peltandra virginica*
Pokeweed	*Phytolacca americana*
Clearweed	*Pilea pumila*
Bracted Plantain	*Plantago aristata*
English Plantain	*Plantago lanceolata*
Common Plantain	*Plantago major*
Nuttall's Milkwort	*Polygala nuttallii*
Cespitose Smartweed	*Polygonum cespitosum*
Mild Water-pepper	*Polygonum hydropiperoides*
Arrow-leaved Tearthumb	*Polygonum sagittatum*
Selfheal	*Prunella vulgaris*
Virginia Meadowbeauty	*Rhexia virginica*
Meadowbeauty hybrid	*Rhexia virginica x mariana hybrid*
Black-eyed Susan	*Rudbeckia hirta*
Curly Dock	*Rumex crispus*
Broad-leaved Arrowhead	*Sagittaria latifolia*

Soapwort	*Saponaria officinalis*
Pitcherplant	*Sarracenia purpurea*
Knawel	*Scleranthus annuus*
Northern Wild Senna	*Senna hebecarpa*
White Campion rea	*Silene latifolia*
Black Nightshade	*Solanum nigrum*
Anisescented Goldenrod	*Solidago odora*
Rough Goldenrod	*Solidago rugosa ssp. r.*
Marsh St. Johnswort	*Triadenum virginicum*
Red Clover	*Trifolium pratense*
Broad-leaved Cattail	*Typha latifolia*
Two-flowered Bladderwort	*Utricularia biflora*
Horned Bladderwort	*Utricularia cornuta*
Purple Bladderwort	*Utricularia purpurea* (some)
Zigzag Bladderwort	*Utricularia subulata*
Common Mullein	*Verbascum thapsus*
Blue Vervain	*Verbena hastata*
White Vervain	*Verbena urticifolia*
Lance-leaved Violet	*Viola lanceolata*
Bog Yellow-eyed Grass	*Xyris difformis*

Rushes

Canadian Rush	*Juncus canadensis*
Common Rush	*Juncus pylaei*
Grass-leaved Rush	*Juncus marginatus*
Brown-fruited Rush	*Juncus pelocarpus*
Forked Rush	*Juncus tenuis*
Path Rush	*Juncus tenuis*

Sedges

| Greenish-white Sedge | *Carex albolutescens* |
| Button Sedge | *Carex bullata* |

Shallow Sedge	*Carex lurida*
Pennsylvanian Sedge	*Carex pensylvanica*
Twig-rush	*Cladium mariscoides*
Toothed Flatsedge	*Cyperus dentatus*
Great Plains Flatsedge	*Cyperus lupulinus*
Shining Flatsedge	*Cyperus sp.* (bipartitus or diandrus)
Threeway Sedge	*Dulichium arundinaceum*
Tawny Cottongrass	*Eriophorum virginicum*
Slender Fimbristylis	*Fimbristylis autumnalis*
White Beaksedge	*Rhynchospora alba*
Brownish Beaksedge	*Rhynchospora capitellata*
Woolgrass	*Scirpus cyperinus*
Common Threesquare	*Scirpus pungens*
Water Bulrush	*Scirpus subterminalis*

Grasses

Redtop	*Agrostis gigantea*
Ticklegrass	*Agrostis hyemalis*
Big Bluestem	*Andropogon gerardii*
Bushy Beard-grass	*Andropogon virginicus*
Sweet Vernal Grass	*Anthoxanthum odoratum*
Smooth Brome	*Bromus inermis*
Orchard Grass	*Dactylis glomerata*
Hairy Crabgrass	*Digitaria sanguinalis* (few)
Quackgrass	*Elytrigia repens*
Weeping Lovegrass	*Eragrostis curvula*
Purple Lovegrass	*Eragrostis spectabilis*
Blunt Mannagrass	*Glyceria obtusa*
Rice Cutgrass	*Leersia oryzoides*
Deertongue	*Panicum clandestinum*
Spreading Panicgrass	*Panicum dichotomiflorum*
Redtop Panicgrass	*Panicum rigidulum*
Velvet Panicgrass	*Panicum scoparium*

Switchgrass	*Panicum virgatum*
Slender Paspalum	*Paspalum setaceum*
Common Reed	*Phragmites australis*
Canada Bluegrass	*Poa compressa*
Little Bluestem	*Schizachyrium scoparum*
Nodding Foxtail	*Setaria faberi*
Yellow Foxtail	*Setaria glauca*
Purpletop	*Tridens flavus*

Ferns & Fern Allies

Foxtail Clubmoss	*Lycopodium alopecuroides*
Southern Bog Clubmoss	*Lycopodium appressum*
Sensitive/ Cinnamon Fern	*Onoclea sensibilis* (some)
Royal Fern	*Osmunda regalis*
Bracken	*Pteridium aquilinum*
Marsh Fern	*Thelypteris palustris*
Netted Chainfern	*Woodwardia areolata*

Resources

To learn more about the topics in this book, the following organizations are a good starting point.

Forest Resource Education Center
370 East Veterans Highway
Route 527
Jackson, NJ 08527
Phone: 732.928.0897
state.nj.us/dep/forestry

New Jersey Department of Environmental Protection
P O Box 402
Trenton, NJ 08625-0402
state.nj.us/dep

Ocean County Historical Society
26 Hadley Ave
PO Box 2191
Toms River, NJ 08754-2191
Phone: 732.341.1880
Fax: 732.341.4372
oceancountyhistory.org

Pinelands Commission
PO Box 7
New Lisbon, NJ 08064
Phone: 609.894.7300
Fax: 609.894.7330
nj.gov/pinelands

Pinelands Preservation Alliance
17 Pemberton Road
Southampton, NJ 08088
Phone: 609.859.8860
Fax: 609.859.8804
www.pinelandsalliance.org

There are some great websites dedicated to enlightening the public about the New Jersey Pine Barrens. They include:

New Jersey Pine Barrens
www.njpinebarrens.com

New Jersey Pines and Down Jersey
www.njpinelandsanddownjersey.com

Piney Power
www.pineypower.com

Selected Bibliography

This bibliography is not inclusive of all work consulted while researching this book, but a selected list of those works that have been of a particular help.

Books

Boyd, Howard P., *A Field Guide to the Pine Barrens of New Jersey* (Medford, NJ: Plexus Publishing, 1991)

Brown, Michael P., *New Jersey Parks, Forests & Natural Areas*, (New Brunswick, NJ: Rutgers University Press, 1992)

Bull, John and John Farrand, Jr., *Audubon Society Field Guide to North American Birds, Eastern Region*, (New York: Alfred A. Knopf, 1977)

Burns, Diane L., *Cranberrries: Fruit of the Bogs* (Minneapolis: Carolrhoda Books, 1994)

Campbell, Carolyn M., M. Peryl King and Martha T. Smith, *Chickaree in the Wall: A History of One Room Schoolhouses in Ocean County*, (Toms River, NJ: Ocean County Historical Society, 1987)

Collins, Beryl Robichaud and Karl H. Anderson, *Plant Communities of New Jersey: A Study in Landscape Diversity* (New Brunswick, NJ: Rutgers University Press, 1994

Collins, Beryl Robichaud and Emily W.B. Russell, *Protecting the New Jersey Pinelands* (New Brunswick, NJ: Rutgers University Press, 1988)

Conant, Roger, *Peterson Field Guide to Reptiles and Amphibians of Eastern and Central North America*, (Boston, MA: Houghton Mifflin Company, 1958)

Eastman, John, *The Book of Swamp and Bog Trees, Shrubs and Wildflowers of Eastern Freshwater Wetlands*, (Mechanicsburg, PA: Stackpole Books, 1995)

Forman, Richard T., *Pine Barrens: Ecosystems and Landscape*, (New Brunswick, NJ: Rutgers University Press, 1979)

Fredeen, Charles, *New Jersey*, (Minneapolis, MN: Lerner Publications Company, 1993)

Harsbberger, John W., *The Vegetation of the NJ Pine Barrens*, (Philadelphia, PA: Christopher Sower Company, 1916)

Kraft, Herbert C., *The Lenape: Archaeology, History and Ethnography*, (Newark, NJ: NJ Historical Society, 1986)

McPhee, John, *The Pine Barrens*, (New York, NY: Farrar Straus Giroux, 1981)

Miller, Pauline S., *Ocean County: Four Centuries in the Making*, (Toms River, NJ: Ocean County Cultural & Heritage Commission, 2000)

Morgan, Ann Haven, *Field Book of Ponds & Streams*, (New York, NY: G. P. Putnam's Sons: 1930)

Mount, Dorothy S., *A Story of New Egypt and Plumsted*, (New Egypt, NJ: New Egypt Historical Society, 1979)

New Jersey Department of Environmental Protection, Division of Parks and Forestry, Forest Resource Service Center, *Trees of New Jersey and the Mid-Atlantic States*

New Jersey Pinelands Commission, *Pinelands Cultural Resource Management Guide*, (New Lisbon, NJ: 1991)

Parnes, Robert, *Canoeing the Jersey Pine Barrens*, (Old Saybrook, CT: Globe Pequot Press, 1978)

Pepper, Adeline, *Tours of Historic New Jersey*, (The New Jersey Tercentenary Commission, 1965)

Peterson, Roger Tory, *A Field Guide to the Birds of Eastern and Central NorthAmerica*, (Houghton Mifflin, 5th edition - April 4, 2002)

Pierce, Arthur D., *Iron in the Pines: The Story of New Jersey's Ghost Towns and Bog Iron* (New Brunswick, NJ: Rutgers University Press, 1957)

Roberts, Russell, *Discover the Hidden New Jersey* (New Brunswick, NJ: Rutgers University Press, 1953)

Robbins, Chandler S., Bertel Bruun and Herbert S. Zim, *Guide to Field Identification: Birds of North America* (Racine, WI: Western Publishing Company Inc., 1966)

Robichaud, Beryl and Murray F. Buell, *Vegetation of New Jersey*, (New Brunswick, NJ: Rutgers University Press, 1989)

Salter, Edwin, *A History of Monmouth & Ocean Counties*, (Bayonne, NJ: E. Gardner & Son, 1890)

Salter, Edwin & George C. Beekman, *Old Times in Monmouth County*, (Baltimore, MD: Genealogical Publishing County, 1980)

Scheller, William G. & Kay, *Off the Beaten Path*, (Guilford, CT: The Globe Pequot Press, 1988)

Schmidt, Marilyn, *Exploring the Pine Barrens of New Jersey*, (Barnegat, NJ: Barnegat Light Press, 1997)

Stokes, Donald and Lillian, *Stokes Field Guide to Birds: Eastern Region* (Little, Brown: 1996)

Stone, Wittmer, *The Plants of Southern New Jersey*, (Boston, MA: Quarterman Publications, Inc.: 1911)

Van Benthuysen, Robert F., *From Surf to Pines: Ocean County, a Bibliography*, (West Long Branch, NJ: Turtle Mill Press, 1990)

Periodicals

New Jersey Outdoors, published by the NJ Fish, Game and Wildlife Division
    Feb. 1951, p 18
    Dec. 1966, p 34
    Feb. 1971, p 32
    Nov/Dec. 1951, p 20-24
    Oct. 1951, p 12-13
    Dec. 1954, p 33

June 1966, p 22-27
May 1965, p 16-19
Sept. 1953, p 9-13
Dec. 1958, p 24-25
July-Aug. 1952, p 9

An Overview of Nonindigenous Plant Species in New Jersey, State of NJ, DEP, February 2004

Newsletters, Brochures, Fliers

Conserve Wildlife newsletter, Spring/Summer 2003, produced by the NJ Dept. of Environmental Protection, Trenton, NJ

Crestwood Village Sun, November 2003 issue, Section B

New Jersey 2003-04 Migratory Bird Regulations, produced by the New Jersey Division of Fish and Wildlife

NJ Fish & Wildlife Digest: A Summary of Rules and Management Information, 2003 Hunting Issue

Pinelands Month Calendar of Events newsletter, produced by the PinelandsPreservation Alliance, Pemberton, NJ

Riparian Forest Buffers, produced by the NJ Forest Resource Education Center, Jackson, NJ, in cooperation with the Barnegat Bay Estuary Program, Toms River, NJ and the Allegheny Society of American Foresters, NJ

Division

Rutgers Cooperative Extension, "Prevent Tick Bites: Prevent Lyme Disease", published by the New Jersey Agricultural Station, pamphlet no. FS443

Websites

Agency for Toxic Substances and Disease Registry, atsdr.cdc.gov/tfacts35.html

Amelia Earhart,
ameliaearhart.com

American Academy of Dermatology,
aad.org/pamphlets/PoisonIvy.html

American Bald Eagle Information,
baldeagleinfo.com

American Forests,
americanforests.org/about_us

American Museum & Natural History,
research.amnh.org/herpetology/amphibia/copyright.php?prompt=1

Aquatic Biologists, Inc.,
aquaticbiologists.com/test/benificalaquaticplants.shtml

Botanical.com,
botanical.com/botanical/mgmh/m/mossph54.html

Connecticut Department of Environmental Protection,
DEP.state.ct.us/earthday/edfunanimals.htm

Cornell Lab of Ornithology,
birds.cornell.edu/programs/AllAboutBirds/BirdGuide/Coopers_Hawk.html

Crater Lake National Park,
nps.gov/crla/notes/vol30d.htm

EMBL Database,
reptile-database.org

Enature.com,
enature.com/flashcard/show_flash_card.asp?recordNumber=BD0046

Hortiplex,
hortiplex.gardenweb.com/plants/help.html

House Rabbit Society,
rabbit.org/faq/sections/orphan.html

How to Identify Snakes,
snakesandfrogs.com/scra/ident/index.htm

Humane Society of the United States,
hsus.org/ace/14573

National Audubon Society,
audubon2.org

National Center for Infectious Diseases,
dc.gov/ncidod/diseases/list_mosquitoborne.htm

National Geographic,
news.nationalgeographic.com

Natural Resources Conservation Service,
plants.usda.gov/cgi_bin/plant_profile.cgi?symbol=COMA7

National Wild Turkey Federation,
nwtf.org

Nature Conservancy,
nature.org/initiatives/programs/birds/features

Natureworks,
nhptv.org/natureworks/whitetaileddeer.htm

New Jersey Department of Environmental Protection,
state.nj.us/dep

New Jersey Department of Health and Senior Services,
state.nj.us/health/cd/f_eee.htm

New Jersey Department of Environmental Protection, Division of Fish
and Wildlife, state.nj.us/dep/fgw/ensp/sommay.htm

New Jersey Waterfowl Association,
njwa.org

Northern Prairie Wildlife Research Center,
npwrc.usgs.gov/narcam/idguide/speeper.htm

Poison Ivy, Oak and Sumac Information Center,
poisonivy.aesir.com

Preflight and Flight Behavior of Canada Geese,
elibrary.unm.edu/sora/Auk/v086n04/p0671-p0681.pdf

Raptor Center, University of Minnesota,
cvm.umn.edu/raptor

Reptile Gardens,
reptile-gardens.com

Salem County Historical Society,
salemcountyhistoricalsociety.com

Switlik Parachute Company,
switlik.com

Tick Biology,
entomology.ucdavis.edu/faculty/rbkimsey/tickbio.html

Tree Guide,
treeguide.com

Trees for Life,
treesforlife.org.uk/tfl.mycorrhizas.html

United States Environmental Protection Agency,
epa.gov

University of Michigan, Museum of Zoology,
animaldiversity.ummz.umich.edu/site/index.html

Virginia Dept of Game and Island Fisheries,
dgif.state.va.us/wildlife/species/display.asp?id=020072

Woodpeckers,
montereybay.com/creagrus/woodpeckers.html

World Owl Trust,
owls.org/Information/breeding.htm

US Dept of Agriculture,
plants.usda.gov/plantguide/pdf/cs_jule.pdf

Endnotes

1. The Quotations Page, quotationspage.com/quote/33522.html (accessed September 26, 2009)
2. Henry Charlton Beck, *Forgotten Towns of Southern New Jersey* (New Jersey: Rutgers State University, 1936), 77-84.
3. Ibid.
4. New York Times obituary, query.nytimes.com/mem/archive-free/pdf?_r= 1&res=9400E7DC133FE233A25755C2A96E9C946496D6CF (accessed September 26, 2009)
5. Amelia Earhart, *Last Flight* (Harcourt, Brace and Company, Inc., 1937)
6. Ibid.
7. Switlik Parachute Company, switlik.com (accessed September 26, 2009)
8. Kraft, Herbert C., *The Lenape: Archaeology, History and Ethnography*, (NJ Historical Society: 1986), 231
9. Pierce, Arthur D., *Iron in the Pines* (Rutgers University Press: 1957)
10. Ibid.
11. Ibid.
12. BBC's Exploration History, bbc.co.uk/history/discovery/exploration/ captaincook_scurvy_01.sht (accessed September 26, 2009)
13. Human Biology Course 121 by Robert J. Huskey and Fred A. Diehl, people.virginia.edu/~rjh9u/vitac.html (accessed May 5, 2004)
14. Ibid.
15. Fact Monster, "Economy," factmonster.com/ce6/us/A0859952.html (accessed September 26, 2009)
16. New Jersey Pinelands Commission, state.nj.us/pinelands/pnrpc.htm (accessed May 5, 2004)
17. Center for Plant Conservation, Missouri Botanical Garden, ridgwaydb.mobot.org/cpcweb/CPC_ViewProfile.asp?CPCNum=2926 (accessed May 5, 2004)
18. M. Grieve, "Spaghnum Moss," Botanical.com: A Modern Herbal, botanical.com/botanical/mgmh/m/mossph54.html (accessed September 26, 2009)
19. Ibid.
20. Boyd, Howard P., *A Field Guide to the Pine Barrens of New Jersey* (Plexus Publishing, NJ: 1991)
21. National Water Summary –Wetland Resources: New Jersey, published

by USGS, 281

22. New Jersey Pinelands Commission, state.nj.us/pinelands/pinecur/
    tcabi78.htm (accessed May 5, 2004)
23. tr-teach.org/resources/news/news percent201999/19990620.html
    (accessed May 5, 2004)
24. US Fish & Wildlife Service, "Wildlife Netting," policy.fws.
    gov/241fw5.html (accessed September 26, 2009)
25. "The Eagle, Our National Emblem," American Bald Eagle Informa-
    tion, baldeagleinfo.com/eagle/eagle9.html (accessed September 26,
    2009)
26. wildturkeybourbon.com/nest/more.htm (accessed May 5, 2004)
27. University of Florida, edis.ifas.ufl.edu/BODY_UW094 (accessed May
    5, 2004)
28. eNature.com, enature.com/flashcard/show_flash_card.
    asp?recordNumber=BD0046 (accessed September 26, 2009)
29. "Florida's Breeding Bird Atlas," Wild Florida, wildflorida.org/bba/
    COHA.htm (accessed May 5, 2004)
30. Cornell Lab of Ornithology, birds.cornell.edu/programs/AllAbout-
    Birds/BirdGuide/Coopers_Hawk.html (accessed May 5, 2004)
31. American Bald Eagle Information, baldeagleinfo.com (accessed Sep-
    tember 26, 2009)
32. The Raptor Center, University of Minnesota, http://www.ahc.umn.
    edu/ahc_content/colleges/vetmed/depts_and_centers/raptor_center/
    index2.cfm?nav=53464&CFID=1223032&CFTOKEN=13682590
    (accessed September 26, 2009)
33. "Migratory Birds," The Nature Conservancy, nature.org/initiatives/
    programs/birds/features (accessed September 26, 2009)
34. "Breeding," World Owl Trust, owls.org/Information/breeding.htm
    (accessed September 26, 2009)
35. Peterson, Roger Tory, *A Field Guide to the Birds of Eastern and Cen-
    tral North America* (Houghton Mifflin; 5th edition - April 4, 2002);
    Stokes, Donald and Lillian, *Stokes Field Guide to Birds : Eastern Region*
    (Little, Brown: 1996)
36. "Big Yellow Taxi," 1969 Siquomb Publishing Co. BMI, Lyrics and
    music by Joni Mitchell, released on the album, *Ladies Of The Canyon*,
    April 1970
37. Junk Science, junkscience.com/ddtfaq.htm (accessed May 5, 2004)
38. "DDT Ban Takes Effect," Department of Environmental Protection,
    epa.gov/history/topics/ddt/01.htm (accessed September 26, 2009)
39. Ibid.

40. Ibid.
41. Junk Science, junkscience.com/ddtfaq.htm (accessed May 5, 2004)
42. Larisa Vredevoe, Ph.D, "Background Information on the Biology of Ticks," Deparment of Entomology, University of California, Davis entomology.ucdavis.edu/faculty/rbkimsey/tickbio.html (accessed September 26, 2009)
43. Ibid.
44. Rutgers Cooperative Extension, "Prevent Tick Bites: Prevent Lyme Disease" published by the New Jersey Agricultural Station, pamphlet no. FS443
45. Ibid.
46. "What You Should Know About...Eastern Equine Encephalitis ," NJ Dept. of Health and Senior Services, state.nj.us/health/cd/f_eee.htm (accessed September 26, 2009)
47. The State of New Jersey, nj.gov/DEP/fgw/ensp/pdf/vernalpool03.pdf (accessed May 5, 2004)
48. nafcon.dircon.co.uk/venomous.htm (accessed May 5, 2004)
49. reptile-gardens.com/reptile/topten.html (accessed May 5, 2004)
50. Collins, Beryl Robichaud and Karl H. Anderson, Plant Communities of New Jersey (New Brunswick, NJ: Rutgers University Press, 1994), 76
51. Ibid.
52. "Native to North America or Introduced?" Cornell University, Ecology and Management – Invasive Plants Program, invasiveplants.net/phragmites/natint.htm (accessed September 26, 2009)
53. "Plant Guide," United States Department of Agriculture, plants.usda.gov/plantguide/doc/cs_assy.doc (accessed September 26, 2009)
54. "Yarrow, " cloudnet.com/~djeans/FlwPlant/Yarrow.htm (accessed May 5, 2004)
55. Poison Ivy, Oak and Sumac Information Center, poisonivy.aesir.com/view/fastfacts.html (accessed September 26, 2009)
56. "Salem Oak," Salem County Historical Society, salemcounty.com/schs/salem_oak.htm (accessed May 5, 2004)
57. "New Jersey Symbols, Tree: Northern Red Oak," SHG Resources, shgresources.com/nj/symbols/tree (accessed September 26, 2009)
58. findarticles.com/p/articles/mi_m1016/is_3_109/ai_109405671 (accessed May 5, 2004)
59. New Jersey Department of Environmental Protection, Division of Parks and Forestry, Forest Resource Service Center, "Trees of New Jersey and the Mid-Atlantic States", 7

60. University of Saskatchewan, "Guide to Birch Trees," gardenline.usask. ca/trees/birch2.html (accessed September 26, 2009)
61. Luanne Berk, "The Ecological Debate: Cloth vs. Disposable," perc.ca/waste-line/articles/diaper.html (accessed September 26, 2009)
62. The Californian, thecalifornian.com/news/stories/20040827/ living/1127311.html (accessed May 5, 2004)
63. Elisa Batista, "The Poop on Eco-Friendly Diapers," *Wired*, April 27, 2004, wired.com/news/technology/0,1282,63182,00.html (accessed September 26, 2009)
64. Nike, nike.com/nikebiz/nikebiz.jhtml?page=27&cat=reuseashoe (accessed April 5, 2004)
65. Lions Clubs International, lionsclubs.org/EN/content/vision_eye-glass_centers.shtml (accessed September 26, 2009)
66. Feeding America, formerly Second Harvert, secondharvest.org/site_content.asp?s=100 (accessed September 26, 2009)
67. The State of New Jersey, state.nj.us/DEP/newsrel/ releases/04_0105gov.htm (accessed May 5, 2004)
68. Ibid.
69. The State of New Jersey, nj.gov/DEP/cleanair/hilite_clean_air.pdf (accessed May 5, 2004)
70. Ibid.
71. online-orienteering.net/orienteering_history (accessed April 5, 2004)
72. NJ Fish & Wildlife Digest 2003 Hunting Issue, 5
73. "Dedicated to the Preservation of a NJ Tradition", pamphlet produced by the New Jersey Waterfowlers Association, Inc., Monmouth Beach, NJ
74. The State of New Jersey, state.nj.us/pinelands/pinecur/ddv.htm (accessed April 5, 2004)
75. All Refer.com Reference, reference.allrefer.com/encyclopedia/A/archery.html (accessed May 5, 2004)
76. NJ Fish & Wildlife Digest, 2003 Hunting Issue, 69
77. List and CMP definition courtesy of the New Jersey Pinelands Commission, revised May 2003
78. List courtesy of the New Jersey Pinelands Commission, revised May 2003

Behind the Scenes

Karen F. Riley has been writing since she was eight years old and nationally published since the age of eleven. She has written for several area newspapers and magazines and is currently at work on her third book. She enjoys interviewing people and capturing their stories in print. Karen, her husband Bill, and their three children – Lisa, Laura and Chris – moved to New Egypt, NJ in 1992, across from the northernmost part of the Pine Barrens.

Andrew Gioulis grew up in a family of skilled artisans. He started out as an illustrator and still incorporates sketches into his work as a graphic designer. Andrew holds a B.S. in Graphic Design/New Media Design from Roberts Wesleyan College and is currently working on his MFA. He has garnered thirty awards for his innovative style. Andrew resides by the Jersey Shore where he can indulge his love of surfing and photography.

KFR Communications, LLC
Karen and Andrew own KFR Communications, LLC, a custom graphic and website design company located on the fringes of the Pine Barrens. More information on their company can be found at www.kfrcommunications.com. They welcome your feedback on *Whispers in the Pines* at info@whispersinthepines.com.

Another Pine Barrens Book from author Karen F. Riley and illustrator Andrew Gioulis...

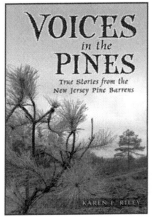

Voices in the Pines: True Stories from the New Jersey Pine Barrens

From the author of *Whispers in the Pines: The Secrets of Colliers Mills*, comes an exciting new non-fiction book that's sure to please! In the spirit of John McPhee's *The Pine Barrens*, author Karen F. Riley roamed the woods, rural communities, and farms of the Pinelands in search of compelling stories. From true life tales of murder and mayhem to inspiring accounts of triumph over adversity and "Pineys" fighting to protect their way of life, *Voices in the Pines* brings the storytelling legacy of the Pine Barrens into the 21st century.

Combining an uncanny ear with a knack for getting perfect strangers to talk freely, Riley takes readers on an engrossing human journey into the heart of the Pines. You'll meet artisans, activists, farmers, educators, local heroes, and regular folks in this collection of true stories, told in the words of those who lived them.

Voices in the Pines: True Stories from the New Jersey Pine Barrens can be ordered online at: www.voicesinthepines.com

To order additional copies of the book you are now holding, please log onto: www.whispersinthepines.com

Karen F. Riley is available for book talks and signings on a variety of topics relating to the Pine Barrens and its people. To schedule, please contact 609.758.1304 or info@voicesinthepines.com